The Christian Lifestyle

The Christian Lifestyle

Reflections on Romans 12—15

by
GEORGE WOLFGANG FORELL

FORTRESS PRESS · Philadelphia

22.71
F76

201580

For
Madeleine Kretschmar Forell
my mother
and a shining example of the power of
the Christian lifestyle

Library of Congress Catalog Card Number 75-13033

ISBN 0-8006-1200-0

4973F75   Printed in U.S.A.   1-1200

Contents

Introduction

What does it mean to live as a Christian at the end of the twentieth century since the birth of Jesus Christ? Some might answer this question by saying: "The same thing today as always. The Christian faith has not changed and therefore the resulting lifestyle has not changed either." The first part of this assertion may well be true; the second part most certainly is not true. A lifestyle results from a combination of factors: (1) who we are, and (2) where we are. For Christians, who they are is determined entirely by their relationship to Jesus Christ. Where they are is determined by history and society, by the culture in which they find themselves.

Unlike most of our ancestors in America and Europe, who lived in a homogeneous world informed by Christian assumptions and values, we live in a world whose assumptions and values come from many different sources, some Christian, some religiously neutral, and some openly and avowedly anti-Christian. For example, "all men are created equal" is a Christian value. Private property as a basic human right is a neutral value. The emphasis on getting the most pleasure out of this life because this is the only life you will ever have is an anti-Christian value. Our culture presents us with a strange mixture of all these values, and the Christian must be able to make distinctions. We must accept some values of our culture because they are a result of or at least congenial to Christianity. We may accept others because Christians can use them and they are not necessarily inimical to the Christian lifestyle. We must reject others because one cannot serve two masters, God and mammon. Where do we turn for help in this complicated and confusing situation? Has there ever been anybody else whose experience was similar to ours and who therefore can help us define the meaning of the Christian lifestlye for our time?

People who lived in Christian countries one hundred or five hundred or even one thousand years ago all lived in far more homogeneous cultures than we do. Even when Roman Catholics disputed Protestants or Christians fought Muslims, there was greater ultimate agreement among the opponents in these battles about the world as creation and God as a benevolent Spirit than we can find in most places today. On the other hand, the world in which Paul lived and wrote was ideologically much like ours. It was a world where religions clashed and people had the option to choose among many lifestyles. Greeks looked down upon barbarians, Romans ridiculed Jews, and city-dwellers scorned country people, and there were many other differences in life-style. We therefore turn to Paul's letter to the Romans for guidance in the development of an attitude toward the culture in which we live and a style of life which is appropriate for people who are called today to live as strangers in a strange land, as a cognitive minority, people with a peculiar perspective among a majority of human beings here and abroad who see the world quite differently.

The Christian lifestyle demands today the courage to be different. We must maintain our point of view and our style of behavior regardless of the requirements of the conventional wisdom. Sometimes what we are will find general approval, sometimes it will be universally rejected. Most of the time it will simply be ignored. We can no longer depend on approval, be frightened by rejection, or dismayed by indifference. Christians are not called to be successful or even impressive—simply to be faithful. It is the apostle Paul in Romans 12-15 who can help us to be just that.

Paul, a servant of Jesus Christ, called to be an apostle, set apart for the gospel of God which he promised beforehand through his prophets in the holy scriptures, the gospel concerning his Son, who was descended from David according to the flesh and designated Son of God in power according to the Spirit of holiness by his resurrection from the dead, Jesus Christ our Lord, through whom we have received grace and apostleship to bring about the obedience of faith for the sake of his name among all the nations, including yourselves who are called to belong to Jesus Christ.

Romans 1:1-6

1

Faith and Life

"Practice makes perfect" is an almost universally accepted proverb. You become good at something by doing it often. Whatever the desired accomplishment, first you perform shakily, but eventually you will do it with some skill. This is as true of driving a car as of playing the piano, of playing golf as of typing.

One might assume that this rule would apply to the appropriation of the Christian lifestyle as well. Indeed, many people, including the Greek philosopher Aristotle, have suggested that becoming morally perfect is an acquired skill which one achieves by persistent practice. Not so the apostle Paul. He spent the first eleven chapters of his letter to the Romans describing and explaining the Christian *faith*. He had summarized it at the beginning in Romans 1:1-6. For him everything characterizing the Christian life depends on the fact that something has happened to the Christian, that he has been "called to belong to Jesus Christ" (Rom. 1:6).

The lifestyle of a person is not a proficiency. It depends on to whom or to what he belongs. If a man belongs to the Hell's Angels he will have one lifestyle, if he belongs to the Black Muslims he will have another; the same would hold true if he belonged to the Mafia or to a team of astronauts. The confusing fact is that we use the term "belong" in quite different senses. "Belong" is used here in a special sense. The way one "belongs" to the Mafia is different from the way one "belongs" to the country club or the Legion Auxiliary. When Paul talks about "belonging to Jesus Christ" he has the first meaning of "belonging" in mind. And if you belong in this sense to anything or anybody, everything has become different. We are no longer talking about a skill which one may acquire or not, exercise or not. We are talking about a lifestyle which determines everything about us and involves all aspects of our life—our skills and our resources, our friends and our family, our job and our leisure.

When Paul talks about the Christian life, he sees it as the way in which a man practices his faith. It is the natural and logical result of faith, of being "called to belong to Jesus Christ," or—as Paul says in describing himself—of being a "servant [or slave] of Jesus Christ" (Rom. 1:1). It has little to do with moral skills or ethical virtuousness. One may be seriously deficient in courage and yet belong to Jesus Christ. Peter displayed his lack of courage by denying Jesus three times, yet showed that he really belonged to Jesus anyway by his tearful reaction to the denial (Matt. 26:69-75). The response was not elegant, but natural and convincing. The history of Christianity is replete with Christians who do morally obtuse things. Their lack of ethical elegance is downright annoying compared with the logical refinement of the great ethicists like Plato or Aristotle, Kant or Nietzsche, or the existentialists of our time.

What all these Christians had in common was not erudition or enlightenment but a profound sense that they were "called to belong to Jesus Christ." Paul's own reaction to incompetence was far from pedagogically inspired when he dropped John Mark from the team after the younger man had failed Paul on his first missionary journey (Acts 15:36-40). But because Paul as well as Barnabas and even John Mark "belong to Jesus Christ" they belonged together even when they went their separate ways. Evidently, the Christian lifestyle is defined not by certain predictable judgments in specific situations but by its total dependence on Jesus, the Christ. It is life in, discipleship to, and fellowship with Jesus the Christ. It is life depending on faith, life whose every aspect rests on the fact of Jesus as the Christ. It is therefore a dynamic style of life, a life constantly formed by faith.

For this reason Paul had to explain the *faith* before he could begin a discussion of the *life*. Without the Christian faith the Christian life is not coherent or ethically significant. Wisdom, courage, moderation, and justice are virtues on which Christians have no exclusive or superior hold. This fact has caused all kinds of trouble in the world when the wisdom of Christians was not commensurate with their power. Everybody would agree that the situation needs improving. However, the key to Christian ethics is not this but rather the awareness that everything depends on one's having been "called to belong to Jesus Christ."

This awareness may be complex or simple, naive or sophisticated, passionate or stolid, highly personal or essentially social, but it is determinative; it is the clue to the Christian life. Persons are committed to the Christian lifestyle because they belong to Jesus Christ in an absolute sense—differently from the way they belong to the Girl Scouts or Boy Scouts, the Rotarians or Lions, the P.T.A. or the Bowling League.

A person is a Christian if he belongs to Jesus Christ. He becomes aware of his being a Christian as he becomes aware of what it means to belong to Jesus Christ. This is an ongoing, lifelong process. Paul tries in his letter to increase his reader's awareness of what it means to belong to Jesus Christ. He cannot *make* them "belong to Jesus Christ," no human being can. He can, however, help them become more conscious of what belonging means, and this is what he is about to do.

As you read the chapters which follow, you might want to ask yourself: "Do I belong to Jesus Christ? Am I a Christian in a different sense than I am a member of the League of Women Voters or the Volunteer Fire Department? Do I belong to Jesus Christ in another way than I belong to the union, the Farm Bureau, the medical association, or the party? What does it mean to say, 'I am a Christian'? Does it mean more to me to be a Christian than to be black or white or red?"

If somebody asked you, "Who are you?" what would first come to your mind? To whom do you really belong? That is Paul's question in chapters 12-15 of his letter. He gives you an opportunity to answer it for yourself.

I appeal to you therefore, brethren, by the mercies of God, to present your bodies as a living sacrifice, holy and acceptable to God, which is your spiritual worship. Do not be conformed to this world but be transformed by the renewal of your mind, that you may prove what is the will of God, what is good and acceptable and perfect.

Romans 12:1-2

2

Life as a Present

One of the most universal religious practices is the performance of sacrifices. People through the ages have been willing to sacrifice their possessions, their comforts, even their loved ones, to their gods. Generally, sacrifice is understood as a bargain with divine power. If the human being is willing to give a present, the divine being is believed to be ready to repay in kind. Thus Agamemnon, the Greek king who was unable to move his ships out of the harbor because of unfavorable winds, was willing to sacrifice his daughter to the gods in order to obtain a change in weather. Indeed, sacrifice is still being practiced. Today one may visit Calcutta and see priests sacrifice goats at the Kali temple in order to influence the goddess Kali on behalf of the person who furnished the present.

Even the Bible reflects this attitude. In the story of the daughter of Jephtha, we are told that this military leader of the Hebrews promised a present to God in order to obtain victory. It was to be "whoever comes forth from the doors of my house to meet me, when I return victorious from the Ammonites" (Judg. 11:31). Eventually, this promise led to his reluctant and tragic sacrifice of his young daughter. While this is probably one of the most poignant tales of sacrifice in the Old Testament, the Bible is full of sacrificial thinking from the story of Abraham and Isaac to the culmination of the New Testament in Jesus' crucifixion.

It is against this background that one must see Paul's call to the Christians in Rome and to all Christians to present their "bodies as a *living sacrifice*, holy and acceptable to God." It is a fascinating transformation and amplification of the entire idea of sacrifice. Generally, the person who made a sacrifice killed and burned something of value and presented this sacrifice to God.

Paul believes that the death of Christ has established an entirely new situation in regard to sacrifice; the old sacrificial system of offering dead animals is abolished. Paul speaks of the believer as the living sacrifice. From now on, to sacrifice does not mean to destroy or kill, but to bring into being, to become alive. The Christian is supposed to see his entire life, his life in the body, his daily existence, as a gift which he can present to God in gratitude for all that God has done for him through Jesus. The Christian life must be a life of gratitude for the mercies of God which Paul has described in the earlier part of the letter. It is the response to the gospel, the good news of God's grace and love.

For the apostle Paul, worship is this presentation of the life of the believer to God. The emphasis is clearly on the entire life—not just part of it. It is the abolition of the distinction between a realm which belongs to God and a realm which belongs to man. If one lives one's life in view of the mercies of God—the deeds of God on behalf of man—then all life must be affected. Life becomes centered in the relationship of God. Life *is* worship.

Most people have bracketed worship into certain short periods of time, perhaps some annual participation in a religious festi-val—going to church at Christmas or Easter—perhaps some weekly attendance at a service of public worship or even daily moments of devotion and prayer. There is nothing wrong with such practices if they are aids to life as worship, if they support and strengthen the Christian in his effort to present his life to God as a living sacrifice. In fact, the practices which are common-ly called "worship" must be evaluated in the light of their func-tion of supporting or hindering the Christian lifestyle, the shaping of all of life in view of God's mercies. One must ask, what kind of ritual for public or private devotion enables people to live their entire life as worship? The question has no simple answer, since each individual experiences distinctive obstacles to the implementation of the Christian lifestyle.

Some people are not aware of the new situation which is the result of the deed of Jesus as the Christ. They have never heard the message in language they are able to understand, or they have the tendency to forget and repress the message. They think that the father of Jesus is just like all the other divine beings in the history of religion, the great computer in the sky who keeps track of the good and evil deeds of mankind and rewards each according to his deserts. This attitude leads to two deplorable reactions. Most people have the gift of looking with great tenderness and charity at their own record of moral achievements. Because they compare themselves with their neighbors, whose lives they judge more harshly, they do not fear the print-out from the heavenly computer. In fact, such people love to go to church to hear God's judgment proclaimed since they have such an optimistic evaluation of their own achievements in comparison with those of their neighbors. Their ability to return their life as a present to God will be strengthened if they are reminded again and again of the grace of God—that while we were still sinners Christ died for our sins. God is no computer.

But there are also some people, Paul, Augustine, and Luther, for example, who are frightened to despair by the judgment of God because they have an unusually realistic view of their own accomplishments and find no comfort in the shortcomings of other human beings who may indeed be worse than they are. They are in despair because of God's purity, power, and justice and contemplate their eternal rejection. Worship for such people must be a powerful and convincing reminder that God loves human beings unconditionally. More emphasis on God's absolute righteousness will only drive such people into despair.

For both kinds of people the most important aspect of formal worship is the proclamation of the gospel, the good news of God's love as revealed in Jesus the Christ. This does not always have to be in learned and logical discourses. A simple hymn or a short prayer may be in certain cases more effective than the most learned speech. The important fact to remember is that formal or informal "worship," as it is commonly called, is only the enabling and strengthening of the real worship which is the daily life of a person.

Worship is not the religious section of human life but rather the time set aside to make it easier for human beings to present all their life as a living present to God. If there is no effect on a person's life then the most elaborate forms of "worship" are from the point of view of the Christian faith a worthless waste of time. Christians must ask: "Is my 'worship' an aid to making my life into a present to God?" If it is not, it must be changed.

*For by the grace given to me I bid every one
among you not to think of himself more
highly than he ought to think, but to think
with sober judgment, each according to the
measure of faith which God has assigned him.
For as in one body we have many members,
and all the members do not have the same
function, so we, though many, are one body
in Christ, and individually members one of
another.*

Romans 12:3-5

3

"Vive la Difference"

For many religious people, and indeed for many Christians, faith is a personal and private matter. They are neither willing nor able to talk about it. If faith belonged in a hidden religious corner of human life which has nothing to do with a person's daily existence, his work and play, the way he earns a living and deals with his family, friends, and fellow workers, it could be treated as a private affair. It would be like one's taste in music. As long as one does not impose it on others, for example, with thousand-watt multispeaker high fidelity equipment, it is really a completely personal matter whether one prefers hard rock to Mozart, or Bach to country and western.

But Paul takes an entirely different position. He thinks an individual is what he believes and that if he believes in Jesus as the Christ he is a different person in all of his human relationships. Therefore, to know that a person believes in Jesus as the Christ is the most important piece of information one could have about him. It is the decisive clue. Because Paul considers faith central, he tries to describe its implications in detail. Faith, he says, relates a person to all other people. It takes him out of his isolation and incorporates the individual into the body of Christ. As members of this body, Christians are responsible for the church and the world. Just as Jesus is the servant-lord, whose lordship is expressed in his service to mankind, so Christians as members of the body of Christ are servants of mankind. Unlike some religious and aesthetic elitists (who once they have found their truth cut themselves off from everybody and pursue their vision), Christians are compelled by their vision to serve mankind as part of their incorporation in Christ.

But then Paul addresses the question, How may this be done?

Is there some standard Christian activity which types people as Christians? Apparently there were some people in Paul's time and presumably in Rome who held the view that all Christians had to act a certain way, that there was a standardized Christian lifestyle. Surprisingly, Paul uses the very image of Christian people as the "body of Christ" to advocate a highly differentiated lifestyle, to suggest that differences among Christians are a good thing. If they are the body of Christ, if they are dependent upon each other like members of a body, then it is vital for the efficiency or even the survival of this body that each part fulfills his own particular responsibility. A healthy body is characterized by the difference in the duties which each member discharges. If every member tries to do the same thing in the same way the body dies.

Paul takes human differences seriously and he believes that Jesus, the Christ, wants to use people with their particular gifts and does not desire a homogeneous mass of standardized and undistinguishable human machines. This might seem like a trivial point were it not for the fact that in the history of the Christian movement the effort to produce standard Christians is far more common than the willingness to allow for variety and particularity. This has resulted in a large number of Christian groups and subgroups, all insisting on a good deal of conformity. Some seek conformity of behavior, others emphasize conformity in belief, still others gather those with similar experiences. All claim that the mark of identification selected by them is crucial. It is because of this stress on uniformity that the unity based on acknowledged and appreciated differences has so far not been achieved.

Paul, often maligned as the spokesman of all rigid orthodoxies from the first century to the present, seems here to welcome variety and complexity. "Having gifts that differ according to the grace given to us, let us use them." And then he proceeds to list some of the central responsibilities which characterize the Christian life: prophecy, service, teaching, exhortation, liberality, administration, performance of acts of mercy. We are accustomed to using the French phrase *vive la difference*, "long live the difference," in a sexist way as being restricted to the physiological differences between men and women. Paul says,

"Long live the difference," precisely because he believes that we are all one body and that differences, all kinds of differences, are essential for the survival of the body. For Paul the wealth of differences which characterize all life should not be ignored or suppressed by Christians but appreciated and used to serve God and all mankind.

Having gifts that differ according to the grace given to us, let us use them: if prophecy, in proportion to our faith; if service, in our serving; he who teaches, in his teaching; he who exhorts, in his exhortation; he who contributes, in liberality; he who gives aid, with zeal; he who does acts of mercy, with cheerfulness.

Romans 12:6-8

4

The Proportion of Faith

For Paul, the Christian lifestyle is characterized by the awareness that Christians depend on each other, that they are responsible for each other. The image of the body—where the hand feeds the mouth, and the lungs and the stomach make it possible for the brain to think and the feet to walk—is for him an illustration of Christian interdependence. Furthermore, the entire body of Christ serves all mankind. It will become apparent later that this even involves responsible obedience to a pagan emperor. But twice in verses 3-8 Paul speaks of "the measure of faith" and the "proportion of faith." It seems as if faith were a quantity of which one can have a little or a lot. In the synoptic Gospels, Jesus apparently speaks of it similarly. Faith can be little or great, and even a little faith can accomplish a great deal (Matt. 8:10, 17:20; Luke 12:28).

Now Paul says that because Christians are responsible for each other they should prophesy in proportion to their faith. This seems to be a warning against religious talk which only confuses and discourages. We live in an age which has observed and studied the close connection between faith and doubt. We have learned that faith is always held against the background of doubt. It is absurd to claim to have faith in a situation in which doubt is no longer possible. Somebody who has never doubted does not seem so much a hero of faith as a credulous fool. But just because the connection between faith and doubt has been perceived more clearly in our age, there is also a tendency to exalt doubt, to make of it a means of grace, as if people were saved by doubt rather than by faith, by distrusting God rather than by trusting him. Religious books considered important by the experts usually cast new doubt on some subject heretofore considered certain.

Even popular religious bestsellers are often bizarre tales about Jesus or the early Christian community.

Even among conservative religious groups the attraction of the weird and occult is prevalent. Isolated passages of the Bible are grasped to spin eccentric tales about the end of the world and the circumstances which will precede and accompany this event. One can almost speak of a form of religious science fiction. Thus the glorification of doubt by one group seems to go hand in hand with the exaltation of credulity and superstition. Small wonder that witchcraft and devil worship seem to have obtained a new lease on life.

Paul's counsel is to speak in proportion to one's faith. To pastors and church school teachers as well as any other Christian called to say something about his faith he suggests: Tell what you know, not what you don't know! It seems like reasonable advice. If somebody who has lost his way driving or hiking asks you for directions you do not tell him the 199 ways of not getting to his goal but rather the one way you know to get there.

Thus, when a person is to bear witness, Paul suggests he should tell people what he believes, i.e., prophesy in proportion to his faith. What does this mean in everyday life? The question What do you believe? comes up in all kinds of strange settings. It is avidly discussed by college students almost as frequently as sex and often more heatedly. It may come up during a break at work or when sitting with friends over a cup of coffee or a glass of beer. It can be triggered by trivial and profound reasons. A newspaper item about some strange religious cult or the sudden death of a person cherished and close may bring up the question of faith. Paul says that when this happens talk in proportion to your faith. What do you really believe? Perhaps you think Jesus was a great man who set an authentic example for all mankind. If you really believe this, say it. It is less than what the Christian tradition considers the whole story, but it is something worth saying.

When the earliest disciples talked about Jesus they would say something like, "We have met a very unusual person and you ought to meet him too." If you have experienced the healing and meaning-giving power of God through Jesus in your life, go ahead and tell people when they ask about your faith. Why should it be wrong to tell what God has done in your life when the subject comes up? Even if it doesn't interest everybody, does everything that people tell about their vacation or the ball game they have seen or their children's success in school interest everybody? Tell what has helped you when the important question of faith comes up. This gives other people the opportunity to tell you what has helped them, and in this way people learn from each other, the body functions by giving mutual support, and our isolation and loneliness is overcome.

Of course, when the subject of faith comes up, you can also tell about the problems of your church. You may wax eloquent about the shortcomings of your pastor, the terrible choir, the chaotic church school, the unfriendly parishioners, but then you are not following Paul's advice to speak in proportion to your faith. Then you will proclaim your irritation and frustration. They are real, too. Paul knew all about such feelings and occasionally proclaimed them to his friends, but here, when he writes the basic advice to people he has not met, he says, proclaim your faith. If you want to help the body of Christ to function, do what you can to build up its members. As you strengthen them they can strengthen you. Speak in proportion to your faith.

Let love be genuine; hate what is evil, hold
fast to what is good; love one another with
brotherly affection; outdo one another in
showing honor. Never flag in zeal, be aglow
with the Spirit, serve the Lord. Rejoice in
your hope, be patient in tribulation, be
constant in prayer. Contribute to the needs
of the saints, practice hospitality.
                                    Romans 12:9-13

5

Love's Content

Less than a generation ago it cost a pittance to mail a postcard across a continent, and that price included the cost of the card. Now you pay eight times as much. We call this development inflation, and it affects food, clothing, and shelter, indeed, all the necessities and luxuries of life. But while everybody is painfully aware of the pervasive reality of economic inflation, there is also a more subtle but equally disturbing verbal inflation at work everywhere. As economic inflation produces worthless money, verbal inflation results in worthless words. We observe it in the supermarket where the large-size tube of toothpaste is really the small size and the giant size is medium large. We see it on television when we are told that "happiness" comes from a certain laxative and life becomes "zestful" from drinking a certain beer.

Some very important words in our language have been devalued by the verbal inflation. *Love* is one of them. Love is a key word in the New Testament, and Paul was apparently aware of the danger of using it in a vague and empty manner. Thus, when he speaks of genuine love, literally nonhypocritical love, he becomes immediately very specific. The "most loving thing" for him is not some vague emotional rationalization of following the path of least resistance and doing what is the least trouble. Paul gives love a specific content. First of all, it means for him the ability and the willingness to tell the difference between good and evil. We live in an age when even some Christian teachers of ethics will tell you "the end justifies the means." If you think it will produce good results you may lie and steal, break and enter, bomb and kill. The result is that anything is permitted if you can persuade yourself that you are doing it with good intentions.

To avoid this trap Paul relates love and truth. Love has to be nonhypocritical, for the God who is love is also truth, and we are not allowed to act as if love were merely a warm feeling which does not make specific demands on us. For Paul it involves "brotherly affection." He lives in a family-oriented society where the brothers and sisters are responsible for each other, support each other in their physical and spiritual needs. The early Christians were known even among their enemies as those who would not only support their own but everybody who was in need.

Paul advocates also a certain way of showing this kind of affection. It is done courteously, respectfully. Christian love fell on evil days when it became charity, because it seems to imply a willingness to help people in need without showing them honor, without respecting them. For Paul, love and respect belong together. Love demands respect for the person loved. What a difference it would make in our charitable efforts if we were always to realize that we cannot really help people if we do not respect them as persons. People complain about welfare because it depersonalizes the recipient; it is relief without respect, help without honor. Paul suggests: "Outdo one another in showing honor."

Of course, none of this is possible, according to Paul, without the help of the Holy Spirit. Paul's ethics is not just good, uplifting advice, but he reminds his readers immediately of the source of all power for the Christian, God the Holy Spirit, who can shine through the love of Christians so that people will notice that they are "aglow with the Spirit." This means to serve the Lord, and here follows a description of what Paul considers to be the Christian lifestyle, the way of life of a loving person.

Strangely enough—but not surprisingly for those who have read Paul's letters—he starts with joy. Love's content includes joy. The gospel is good news and the Christian message is "joy to the world" and "tidings of great joy." We sometimes think that the proper mood for people living towards the end of the twentieth century is pessimism and despair. We are surrounded by more or less scientific prophets of doom who make a mood of joy and happiness seem naive and strangely out of place. If we remember that Paul has been shipwrecked, beaten, stoned, imprisoned, and is on his way to his eventual execution, we will not dismiss his emphasis on joy as naiveté growing out of the sheltered life he has lived.

Paul says, Christians may rejoice because they have hope. It isn't because of their glorious past but rather because of their graceful future that they may rejoice. They are God's pilgrim people on the march into God's tomorrow. For them existence in this world is not meaningless decay but a purposeful journey towards life. For people in our day so frightened by the future that they clutch anything that will remind them of the good old days, even if it is an old magazine cover, pre-stereo music record, an antique collection, Paul's hope may seem peculiar—but it is part of the content of the love. And it enables him to say: "Be patient in tribulation." A long journey is never without its difficulties. There are the experienced travelers who know that patience is the only way to survive without losing one's mind—and there are the novices who get nervous when the plane doesn't start on time or if they have to wait for twelve other planes before it is their turn to take off. Paul suggests patience for the traveler on his pilgrimage, and while he is waiting he might as well pray: "Be constant in prayer." What kind of persons might you and I be if all the hours we have used fretting and worrying while waiting in offices and terminals, standing in long lines, and expecting people to meet us had been used by us for prayer and meditation? It staggers the imagination.

And then Paul concludes: "Contribute to the needs of the saints, practice hospitality." The Greek *koinonountes* means "share" or "participate" in the needs of your partners on this long journey into God's future. Such a journey can be dull and depressing; or it can be a joyful and happy experience. We are all in this together—and if our love is genuine it can be fun.

Bless those who persecute you; bless and do
not curse them. Rejoice with those who
rejoice, weep with those who weep. Live in
harmony with one another; do not be haughty,
but associate with the lowly; never be
conceited. Repay no one evil for evil, but take
thought for what is noble in the sight of all.
If possible, so far as it depends upon you,
live peaceably with all. Beloved, never avenge
yourselves, but leave it to the wrath of God;
for it is written, "Vengeance is mine, I will
repay, says the Lord." No, "if your enemy is
hungry, feed him; if he is thirsty, give him
drink; for by so doing you will heap burning
coals upon his head." Do not be overcome
by evil, but overcome evil with good.

Romans 12:14-21

6

The Style of Love

The American anthropologist Ruth Benedict showed in her widely read book *Patterns of Culture* that preliterate tribes have developed vastly different styles of organizing their lives. Some tribes emphasize competition, others build their lives around witchcraft and the conviction that nothing happens without the use of good or evil magic. Still others try to avoid all tension-producing situations and live with a minimum of friction and confrontation.

It might be possible to characterize some developed civilizations by their lifestyles. North Americans seem to emphasize competition from cradle to grave, trying to outdo each other in everything from fashionable baby carriages to equally fashionable hearses, obsessed by records as to who can run faster, eat more pies, or sit on flagpoles longer. A little boy will say to his friend, "My father can beat your father." Political leaders never tire of assuring their constituents that "we are the richest, the most powerful—second to none."

If competition and braggadocio characterize American lifestyle, one could say after reading Solzhenitsyn's book *The Gulag Archipelago* about the Soviet penal system that consciously promoted terror characterizes the lifestyle of that country. Jails, prison camps, and executions are not so much punishment for offenders as the means to produce a pervasive mood of terror which makes this kind of empire possible. The Japanese seem to build their life around the concept of honor and shame, emphasizing the importance of keeping or losing face. Some Latin peoples stress the notion of machismo, male comradeship and invulnerability.

Against this background we note that for Paul the Christian

lifestyle is built around love. Love is the clue to our relationship to fellow believers, and at the same time it determines the Christian attitude towards all people. "Bless those who persecute you." Pray for them and speak well of them. Love goes out to those who try to make our lives miserable. And again Paul becomes specific: "Rejoice with those who rejoice, weep with those who weep." Jesus was able to do both. He went to the marriage feast at Cana and rejoiced with those who rejoiced—to a fault, some would say, when he helped the embarrassed host by supplying large quantities of wine. And when he found Mary and Martha in tears after the death of their brother Lazarus he wept with those who did weep, a loving action which does not fit the tearless hero we tend to admire.

We often have trouble with both these Pauline injunctions. We feel jealous of the happiness of others and threatened by their sadness. We will not speak even to the widow of a good friend who has died because, even though speaking well of him might comfort her, speaking of him at all may make us sad.

To love means to enter into the life of others, their joy and pain. And the style of love implies what the Quakers call a "sense of the meeting," a concern with harmony rather than winning points. This has all sorts of implications. Democracy, for example, can be the rule of the majority trampling the minority underfoot. It can also be the patient development of a consensus of harmony which takes into consideration the interests of the minority. We tend to practice the former, while Paul advocates the latter. It is more important to win a friend than an argument. Yet in the church we have seen the spectacle of Christians defaming, excluding, and even killing other Christians because of their opinions. It is still a popular way to gain friends among the like-minded haughtily to question the sincerity of those who do not agree with us. No longer able to kill, we malign, even fire them if they hold offices in the church. "Never be conceited," says Paul, but religious conceit can be the most destructive of all.

"Repay no one evil for evil." Nothing goes as directly against our instincts as this injunction. From the trivial reaction of slowing the car when somebody blows his horn immediately after the light has changed, to the grudge held for decades against a brother who may have injured us at one time, repaying evil for evil is probably the favorite pastime of the human race. Paul says, "Don't!" How can we go against such a basic human drive? Paul's suggestion is: "Trust God!" God is just, he will see to it that justice is done. For those who do not believe in God's justice, it may be impossible to avoid taking justice into their own hands. For God's people such an effort is foolish and idolatrous. This even applies to their attitude towards law enforcement. They will expect the law to be designed to prevent further crimes rather than revenge society or the injured individual. This is God's privilege alone.

But Paul goes further: "If your enemy is hungry, feed him; if he is thirsty, give him drink." Paul quotes here the language of the Old Testament (Prov. 25:21). He suggests that for Christians not vengeance but the idea of winning the enemy over by acts of kindness and love should be uppermost. Paul summarizes: "Do not be overcome by evil, but overcome evil with good."

Because the Christian knows God through Jesus, the Christ, he does not have to play God in his relationship to other human beings. He is freed to be human. To overcome evil with good becomes the theme of his life. The few illustrations Paul has given in these verses serve only as pointers; the key to the Christian lifestyle is to be freed from self-concern, the need to be appreciated, revenged, feared, even right! Free to be present for the other person, rejoicing, weeping, supplying physical and spiritual needs. Paul seems to think that this is the way the Spirit of God enables His people to live.

It may sound too simple. But remember the source before you write it off as foolishness. Try it for a day or a week. What can you lose? Would it work in business? I don't know. Perhaps modern business is based on such deceit that what Paul has to say is irrelevant to the capitalist system. That the Christian could undermine the system of terror Solzhenitsyn has described is so obvious to the defenders of this style of life that they oppose the Christian faith with all their resources. But this may only show the inadequacy of some of the lifestyles offered to people today. Indeed, Paul and the style of love may be irrelevant to modern capitalism and communism. This may imply that these systems are dehumanizing and irreconcilable with the true welfare of human beings today.

Let every person be subject to the governing authorities. For there is no authority except from God, and those that exist have been instituted by God. Therefore he who resists the authorities resists what God has appointed, and those who resist will incur judgment.

Romans 13:1-2

7

The Source of Authority

Few passages in the Bible have had as far-reaching an influence on the world in which we live as these two verses in Paul's letter to the Romans: "Let every person be subject to the governing authorities. For there is no authority except from God, and those that exist have been instituted by God. Therefore he who resists the authorities resists what God has appointed, and those who resist will incur judgment." These words have largely determined the Christian attitude towards the state.

Scholars are still debating why Paul brought up the Christian political obligation at this particular point in his letter. He never mentions the subject in any of his other surviving writings. Did he suspect that the Christians in Rome were particularly anti-establishment? Did he feel that a letter to the capital of the empire should address the question of the Christian and the state? Or did he, as some have suggested, feel that having rejected any right to revenge for Christians and having exhorted them to overcome evil with good, he now had to call attention to the power which in this world restrains criminals and maintains "law and order"?

Those who are familiar with Paul's missionary career know that he had found the Roman Empire a help in his work. Roman armies and navies had made the roads and sea-lanes relatively safe and had restrained highwaymen and pirates. For a constant traveler like Paul this was reason to be grateful.

His personal experiences with Roman government officials had also been positive. In Greece the Roman proconsul Gallio had ejected Paul's accusers since he did not want to get involved in a religious dispute (Acts 18:12-15). Later in Caesarea Paul appealed to the emperor before Governor Festus and thus escaped a religious trial in Jerusalem (Acts 25:10-12). Small wonder that Paul thought highly of the Roman government.

But there is more to this passage than Paul's personal opinion about the government of his time. He proposes a Christian approach to politics which insists that political authority is a gift of God and the means God uses to rule the world. Just as God feeds infants through mothers, provides food for mankind through farmers, educates the ignorant through teachers, heals the sick through doctors, so he keeps order in the world through "governing authorities."

Paul's claim is that this world is God's world, but God uses human beings to accomplish his purposes. They can be strange servants indeed. Isaiah writes, "Thus says the Lord to Cyrus his anointed, Cyrus whom he has taken by the hand to subdue nations before him and undo the might of kings" (Isa. 45:1 NEB). Cyrus was a Persian king, but that did not keep God from giving him authority to accomplish His purposes. The fact that God gives a person authority to do something He wants to accomplish does not necessarily make him His child. God may use peculiar instruments to accomplish His plans. He once used an ass to restrain a prophet (Num. 22:22ff.).

Paul thinks it is important for Christians to understand that this world is not a "tale told by an idiot, full of sound and fury, signifying nothing"; it is God's world in which His will is done. Frequently this may be hard to see from our point of view. Paul therefore reminds us, "There is no authority except from God."

This tells us two important facts about the Christian view of human authority. Authority is not of itself bad. We live in an age when the flagrant abuse of power has created a crisis of authority. This affects every form of rule, from the influence of parents in the home to the jurisdiction of the United Nations in the world. While no institution is untouched by this crisis, political authority has become particularly suspect. Paul's statements remind us that while presidents and vice-presidents may betray our confidence, the need for governing authority remains, because human beings need order to survive. The anarchy advocated by some is in reality even more obviously the tyranny of the strong against the weak. Wherever political authority breaks down in a community it is the weak who suffer most.

They cannot afford personal bodyguards and will be abused by everybody. Even though some representatives of "governing authority" may be weak or corrupt (and so should be replaced) governmental authority is God's way of maintaining relative peace and justice in a world where human sin threatens our survival and where the weak are at the mercy of the strong.

But Paul also insists that all authority, especially political authority, depends on God. It is not "autonomous," i.e., independent of God and free from His rule. In our time, whenever the church in assembly says a word about peace or justice, some politician who doesn't happen to agree with the position taken will claim that the church should only speak about the life to come and that politicians alone have the right to make pronouncements about the affairs of this world. It is obvious that the personal political opinion of a clergyman or any other Christian is just that, and as valid as the personal political opinion of a lawyer, a football star, a nuclear scientist, or a parking-lot attendant. But when the church has studied a subject, discussed it, and voted on it in an assembly of democratically chosen representatives, its statements are as legitimate and important as all other statements arrived at in a similar fashion.

Precisely because there is "no authority except from God, and those that exist have been instituted by God," it is of the greatest importance that all people, especially Christians, take a responsible interest in such authority. It is love's obligation not to abandon the political realm but to participate actively, in order to make it work on behalf of the best interests of all human beings. To say, "Politics is a dirty business," and to abandon it is irresponsible. If God is willing to become involved in politics by establishing governing authorities, Christians can do their share to see that these authorities govern in the interest of the people for whom they were instituted. Politics may be dirty business; it's not going to become cleaner if Christians refuse to help clean it up.

For rulers are not a terror to good conduct, but to bad. Would you have no fear of him who is in authority? Then do what is good, and you will receive his approval, for he is God's servant for your good. But if you do wrong, be afraid, for he does not bear the sword in vain; he is the servant of God to execute his wrath on the wrongdoer.

Romans 13:3-4

8

The Limit of Authority

Paul's insistence that Christians ought to be law-abiding citizens is based upon a positive understanding of the nature and duty of the "governing authorities." When he assures his readers that "rulers are not a terror to good conduct, but to bad," he is thinking of a government which upholds the law in a fair and just manner. Soon he and other Christians caught in Nero's bloody persecutions found out that this assumption may not always be justified. It was their experience with an unjust government which led later Christian writers, for example, the author of the Book of Revelation, to speak of authority in quite a different way. In Revelation 13 the Roman government is the "beast from the sea" which is "allowed to make war on the saints and to conquer them" (Rev. 13:7). Now indeed it has become a terror to good conduct rather than bad, and the Book of Revelation calls for the "endurance and faith of the saints" (Rev. 13:10).

Christians reading both Romans and Revelation have often wondered about the limits of authority. At what point must one say "no" to an authority which is instituted by God? It is hard to give an answer which will meet all situations—but the injunction that "we must obey God rather than men" (Acts 5:29) applies here. It is unsafe to go against one's conscience, and Christians must not let their respect for authority make them into tools of injustice, oppression, or cruelty.

Most of us seem only too ready to yield our personal responsibility to authority, any authority. We like to get off the hook and want someone in authority to blame for our irresponsible, evil, and cruel actions. In a recent book, *Obedience to Authority: An Experimental View*, the social psychologist Stanley Milgram tells about an experiment which showed that most of us would rather follow orders than disobey authority, even if the authority tells us to treat people cruelly and inflict pain. Milgram invited his experimental subjects, who were ordinary people, to teach random word pairs to learners by delivering a series of increasingly more powerful electric shocks for every wrong answer given by the learner. Over 60 percent of his subjects did exactly what they were told, even though the [pretended] shocks ranged up to 450 volts and were described to the subjects as dangerously severe; and even though the learners, who were trained actors, would complain about the pain beginning at 150 volts and scream, begging to be released, from the 300 volt level upwards. Apparently the "scientific" nature of the experiment and the authority which science enjoys in our time immunized the subjects to their ordinary human responsibility. As at one time everything that was done for religious reasons seemed defensible, so today any act that is claimed to be "scientific" enables us to suspend ordinary human judgment.

By giving clear reasons for obedience to governing authority, Paul encourages us to keep on thinking, even if we are commanded to act by what we consider a legitimate authority. The question we must constantly ask is: "Does what we are about to do support good conduct?" The moral question is not suspended by the commands of an authority. It must be constantly kept in mind.

Unfortunately, Paul has not always been interpreted in this way. Romans 13:1 and 2 has been read without reference to 13:3 and 4. The result has often been tragic and made many Christians into thoughtless robots defending government and the status quo. There are still some who will use Romans 13 to attack the courageous positions of a Dietrich Bonhoeffer or Eivind Berggrav, who opposed Hitler during World War II. Similarly, some Christians uncritically support the statement "My country, may she ever be right, but right or wrong my country." Some of the apologists for war criminals say that these people are not guilty because they were merely obeying orders from higher authority—the very defense used by the Nazi war criminals at Nuremberg.

It is not only in regard to political authority or the power of the state that these verses from the thirteenth chapter of Romans are important. As Milgram's experiment shows, there are other "authorities" that people will obey unquestioningly in order to avoid facing the need for a personal answer to the question of what is "good" conduct and what is "bad." In school, students and teachers often blindly follow the authority of the peer group. Many medical doctors are led like sheep by their professional associations. Some labor union members accept benightedly the authority of their leaders. No human being seems safe from the danger of worshiping "authority" rather than God. The question of what is "good" and "bad" is ignored or repressed.

Nowhere is this tendency to blindly follow authority more deplorable than in the church. Yet anybody who has ever attended a congregational meeting has seen the idolatry of authority in action. First of all, few members even come to such meetings—any excuse will do to absent themselves. Those few—often less than 10 percent of the eligible membership—who do turn up tend to go along with authority. The question of "good" and "bad" is hardly ever confronted. Some shallow sense of loyalty stifles any discussion. No wonder that in the present quest for the recovery of a moral foundation for our life together the voice of the church is muffled. It too seems to have sold out to the various authorities that allow us to suspend judgment about the question of "good" and "bad" and concentrate on more pragmatic concerns—such as, "Will it work?" or perhaps, "Is it modern, profitable, scientific?" We should remember that the sale of indulgences in the sixteenth century was eminently profitable and had been endorsed by all the authorities; but, as Luther pointed out, it was simply wrong.

If we want to understand love's political obligation, it is not enough to quote Paul's endorsement of the governing authorities as deriving from God. We must also remember that the limit of all authority is the question "Whom does it serve?" If it does not serve human beings, it is evil, since "the Sabbath was made for man and not man for the Sabbath." Authority, every kind of authority, is justified only as it serves the earthly welfare of human beings. "For rulers are not a terror to good conduct, but to bad."

Therefore one must be subject, not only to avoid God's wrath but also for the sake of conscience. For the same reason you also pay taxes, for the authorities are ministers of God, attending to this very thing. Pay all of them their dues, taxes to whom taxes are due, revenue to whom revenue is due, respect to whom respect is due, honor to whom honor is due.

Romans 13:5-7

9

The Christian Approach to Politics

Paul gives two reasons that all people should support their government. The first, he says, is "to avoid God's wrath." He is convinced that God will punish those who fail to do their duty towards the authorities which he calls "the servant" God has established for the benefit of all mankind. But Paul adds that we should support our government "also for the sake of conscience." It is this same conscience, which according to an earlier chapter of this letter (2:14-15), tells all human beings the demands of God's law. Paul wrote: "When Gentiles who have not the law do by nature what the law requires, they are a law to themselves, even though they do not have the law. They show that what the law requires is written on their hearts, while their *conscience* also bears witness."

A person who knows nothing of the Christian gospel may be a fair judge, an honest governor, a hardworking, competent, and compassionate member of a legislative body. This should not surprise us, for the law as a guide to the earthly welfare of mankind is available to everybody. Christians sometimes act as if the Golden Rule were a uniquely Christian injunction and the center of the New Testament proclamation. There is probably no major religious tradition which does not cherish some form of this rule, and the philosopher Kant claimed that this rule, which he reworded and called the "categorical imperative," was available to all human beings through reason.

Thus everybody has access to the law, and politics, which benefits humanity only if it is governed by law, is the domain of reason. The Christian approach to politics must therefore be reasonable. This is what Paul suggests: "Pay all of them their dues, taxes to whom taxes are due, revenue to whom revenue is due." Some scholars claim that Paul makes here a distinction between direct and indirect taxes, others again say that one term describes the tribute demanded by a foreign master-nation, the other ordinary local taxation. Whatever the distinction, Paul insists that Christians ought to handle the matter of taxation in a responsible and reasonable way; indeed, that their participation in political life should be directed by conscience.

Here he reflects his Hellenistic tradition. The Greek-speaking people in the Mediterranean world believed with the Jewish philosopher Philo: "Conscience is born with every soul and makes its abode with it, nor is it wont to admit herein anything that offends. Its property is ever to hate the evil and love the good. This same thing is at once both accuser and judge."

Reason and conscience are available to all people, and appeals to reason and conscience are universally understood. Political decisions should be made with their help, avoiding both cynicism and sentimentality. When Paul stood before Festus (Acts 25) he had a sentimental option. He could say piously, "I'll leave it all to God," and be judged in Jerusalem. He also had a cynical option; he could say, "All governments are corrupt, and Festus has probably been bribed by my enemies," and do nothing. Instead he appealed to conscience—"I have done no wrong"—and to reason—"I appeal to Caesar." As a result of this skilled political act his ministry was extended for years.

It is this politically alert attitude which distinguishes Paul from many modern Christians who are either cynical or sentimental about politics. Some say, "Politics is corrupt," or, "All politicians are rascals." The effect of such talk is that people refuse to participate in the political processes which enable them to "throw the rascals out." Still others are sentimental about government, piously assuming that all officials are equally honest and that the citizen is bound to support them whether they uphold the law or not. Accepting bad rulers as divine punishment, they fail to use their reason and conscience to make politics serve the interests of all citizens.

Paul advocates reliance on conscience, and Christians ever since have appealed to conscience when confronted by unjust rulers or unjust laws. Luther at Worms appealed to conscience, saying that it was not safe for him to recant, though commanded to do so by the emperor, because one must not go against one's conscience. Similarly, people have left religious oppression in one continent and moved to another for conscience's sake. Others again have disobeyed racist laws in their native land because obeying them would have been against their conscience.

It is apparent that conscience does play an important part in the Christian approach to politics. But what does this mean in the light of the emphasis on love, which Paul earlier claimed to be the key to the Christian life? What happens when you mix love, conscience, and reason? The result may very well be *justice*. Many students of ethics have suggested that justice is love distributed. If a person wants to show love to all people he will act justly. A simple illustration may help. If you have one apple and three children you love, it is a sign of your love that you will give each one a third of the apple. But this is also justice.

If we design a society in which every person is treated with love in the way in which Paul uses this term earlier (Rom. 12:9-13), where he combines love and respect, we will have a just society. Justice is not the enemy of love but the application of love to society. If the Christian approach to ethics is faith active in love, the Christian approach to politics is love active in justice.

The Christian approach to politics demands not the sentimental disregard of reason but a painstaking and loving application of reason to the affairs of all human beings. This means one must study issues before taking a stand, trying to understand the conflicting positions, listening carefully. When this has been done, one must act according to one's conscience. Conscience has the word *science* in it. It has something to do with knowledge. The very importance of conscience demands the effort to know. That applies to issues as controversial and complicated as abortion and the death penalty, war and revolution, ecology and racism. We may not be able to master all the issues, but if we are to appeal to conscience we must make an effort to know. Voluntary ignorance is escape from Christian responsibility. Far from being bliss, it may be sin.

Owe no one anything, except to love one another; for he who loves his neighbor has fulfilled the law. The commandments, "You shall not commit adultery, You shall not kill, You shall not steal, You shall not covet," and any other commandment, are summed up in this sentence, "You shall love your neighbor as yourself." Love does no wrong to a neighbor; therefore love is the fulfilling of the law.
                                        Romans 13:8-10

10

Love and Law

Sometimes people play a game called "Association." You say one word and your partner says the word that immediately comes to mind, the word he associates with the one you have offered. It can be interesting and occasionally funny or sad, because people might reveal more of themselves with one little word than with a long and well-prepared speech.

If we were to play this game and I would say "love," what would come to your mind? Hate, mother, Jesus, God, country, sex? Perhaps all of these, but certainly not "law." We simply do not associate love and law. Conversely, if I were to say "law," you might think of order, justice, courts, police, lawyers, but hardly of love.

The strange thing about Paul is that he associates law and love. He says, "Owe no one anything, except to love one another; for he who loves his neighbor has fulfilled the law." And a little later: "Love is the fulfilling of the law." By so closely associating love and law Paul tells us something significant about the Christian understanding of both these words.

In the Bible law is a good thing. The Hebrew word most frequently translated as "law" is *Torah*. It occurs 217 times in the Old Testament. The psalmist sings of it: "Oh, how I love thy law! It is my meditation all the day." And he says that the man whose "delight is in the law of the Lord" and who "meditates on the law day and night" is blessed (Ps. 1). This is how Paul has been taught to think of the law. It is the most wonderful gift God has given his people. It is the gift Israel is called to share with the Gentiles, "For out of Zion shall go forth the law, and the word of the Lord from Jerusalem" (Mic. 4:2). But when he tries to summarize this law which God has given to Israel, he comes up with the statement: "The commandments, 'You shall not commit adultery, You shall not kill, You shall not steal, You shall not covet,' and any other commandment, are summed up in this sentence, 'You shall love your neighbor as yourself.' "

For Christians, Paul says every law must be the expression of love, the kind of love that God constantly shows to us and that we are privileged to pass on to our neighbors. A person who takes the law absolutely seriously will be a loving person. There are probably few suggestions in the New Testament which are harder to grasp for contemporary people. For us the law is often the way in which we avoid being loving people. When we hate somebody we drag him before the law. When we do not want to pay our share for the support of our civilization, we try to find a clever lawyer who may discover a law that enables us not to pay taxes. Indeed, lawyers, the people who are most expert in the law, have a bad reputation among most people. When a person is hard and unloving in his relationship to people we call him a legalist, a person who goes by the law.

The reason for this negative view of the law in our time is precisely that we have lost the connection between law and love. Unlike Martin Luther, we no longer see that the Ten Commandments are a way to help us show love. Luther explained the commandment "Thou shalt not kill" in his *Small Catechism* as saying not only that "we should not do our neighbor any bodily harm or injury" but also that "we should assist and comfort him in danger and want." Or when talking about bearing false witness he was not satisfied to warn against lying, betrayal, and slander of our neighbor, but said we should "apologize for him, speak well of him, and put the most charitable construction on all his actions." He treated all the commandments in this way, making it clear that "the fullness of the law, therefore, is love," as Paul says if we translate verse 10 literally.

Thus the Christian when confronted by any law should, according to Paul, give it the most loving interpretation possible. He should ask, in the light of God's love to us, what does it mean to obey the law of my country, my state, my community? Even the laws governing our life together in a family or in a school or at a place of business, the laws guiding the behavior of the professions, of doctors, real-estate agents and insurance salesmen, and the myriad of other professions and jobs, should be looked at from the point of view of love. If your company makes a law saying you should wear a hard hat at a building site, look at it from the point of view of love rather than convenience, and thousands of accidents could be prevented. If the law says to fasten your seat belt in the car, and the car starts making strange noises when you don't, forget the many wisecracks about knuckleheads in the capital and the many clever devices for circumventing the intent of the buzzer, and ask yourself instead, "What does love require of me?" Instead of putting a false wall between love and law, Christians should learn from Paul to see all laws in the light of love and interpret them lovingly.

But if we do that, one other fact will become obvious. In spite of our best intentions and efforts, it is impossible to obey the law, interpreted by love, perfectly. It is this understanding of the law which makes us aware of what Paul has said earlier in this letter: "No human being will be justified in [God's] sight by works of the law, since through the law comes knowledge of sin" (Rom. 3:20). Obedience to the law in the light of love not only makes us better citizens but also opens our eyes to our need for the forgiveness of sins, a new beginning Jesus Christ is willing to give us every day, even though we have failed, "have sinned and fallen short of the glory of God" as Paul puts it.

Only if we take the law seriously, namely, see it in the light of love, can it accomplish its most important task, to drive us to Christ. When we dissolve the connection between law and love, the law becomes superficial and useless, both politically and theologically. It enables us to evade our responsibilities to our neighbor, and it does not reveal our profound need of a savior. When we follow Paul and Luther connecting law and love, the law will make us better citizens and at the same time prepare the way for our realization that Jesus, the Christ, is our Lord and Savior. Only when the profound relationship between love and law is seen can we say: "For we hold that a man is justified by faith apart from works of law" (Rom. 3:28).

Besides this you know what hour it is, how it is full time now for you to wake from sleep. For salvation is nearer to us now than when we first believed; the night is far gone, the day is at hand. Let us then cast off the works of darkness and put on the armor of light; let us conduct ourselves becomingly as in the day, not in reveling and drunkenness, not in debauchery and licentiousness, not in quarreling and jealousy. But put on the Lord Jesus Christ, and make no provision for the flesh, to gratify its desires.

Romans 13:11-14

11

The Significance of Hope

A psychiatrist who was a prisoner in a Nazi concentration camp towards the end of World War II reported later that he had discovered how to tell which prisoners had a chance to survive the ordeal and which would likely perish. Some would describe in detail the wonderful parties which they had enjoyed before the war, the meals they had eaten, the good times they once had. Others would talk in equal detail about the marvelous parties and meals they planned to have when they were freed. The psychiatrist later noted that those who were obsessed by the past were likely to die, while those who were concerned with the future were likely to live.

For human beings hope is not a luxury; it is an essential ingredient of life. If one has no hope one is desperate, a word which means literally to be without hope. For Paul, hope was one of the three major elements of the Christian life. It belonged with faith and love to the basic equipment of the Christian. While most of us appreciate Paul's emphasis on faith and love, modern Christians seem to be able to do very little with hope. When we hear the phrase "Today is the first day of the rest of your life" we feel threatened. Time is running out on us. Soon we will be dead. We tend to be more concerned with the past than with the future, the good old days rather than the promise of tomorrow. Paul had hope and his reason was simple: "Salvation is nearer to us now than when we first believed." Today you are one day closer to the day when Jesus the Christ will be revealed to all people, indeed, to the entire universe, as Lord of lords and King of kings. "The night is far gone, the day is at hand."

The German philosopher Ernst Bloch claims that Sigmund Freud was wrong because he emphasized people's dreams about the events of their past. Bloch insists that the reliable clue to a person is not what he dreams at night about his past but rather what he dreams during the day about his future. What are your daydreams? What is your hope for the future? It reveals what kind of person you are, your real interests.

Paul dreamed about the coming day of Jesus Christ; like all the early Christians he could hardly wait for tomorrow. But he did not only dream about it; he lived and he wanted all Christians to live, in the light of this new day. He wanted them to anticipate the coming kingdom of God by living as citizens of this kingdom even now. Some of the imagery he borrowed from the experience of a cultured Greek among the "barbarians." When living away from Athens and under foreign rule, it would be possible for a Greek to "go native," to forget his education and culture, his responsibility to be a representative of the Greek lifestyle. Instead, the ancient Greeks were so faithful to their culture that they persuaded the barbarians to adopt Greek ways, language, poetry, even Greek names for their gods, and made Greeks out of the very people who had conquered them in battle. The Mediterranean world of Paul's time was a Greek-speaking world because the Greeks had behaved as citizens of Greece and persuaded Romans and Egyptians, Persians and Syrians to adopt Greek ways.

Paul hoped that Christians might do the same if they would act as citizens of heaven and "cast off the works of darkness and put on the armor of light." Mankind would pay attention, and many of them might get in on this great day that was coming. It was this incredible confidence, this audacious hope, which made Paul into the triumphant apostle to the Gentiles. He knew that the future belonged to Christ, and as a result nothing could possibly shake his hope. He could comfort his jailer in Philippi while he himself was a prisoner in the jail, and he could write comforting letters to his congregations all over the Mediterranean world while a prisoner of Emperor Nero.

One of the problems that faces Christians in our day is the apparent loss of hope. We seem forever to be looking backward, hankering for the good old days instead of looking confidently to the future. We seem to want to return to "Egypt," which is at least familiar to us, rather than go forward facing the dangers of the "desert" because the "promised land" is unknown and therefore threatening.

The result has been that hope, once the trademark of the Christian movement and an essential feature of the Christian lifestyle, has been usurped by other movements. The conviction that tomorrow belongs to us, that the night is far gone, the day is at hand, is more frequently heard from Communists than from Christians. They seem to believe that whatever may be wrong with the present, the future belongs to them. This is why a Russian visiting the United States some years ago could strike terror into the hearts of many Americans by claiming, "Your children will live under Communism." He apparently had hope— many Christians seem to have abandoned it.

This forsaking of hope as an essential aspect of the Christian lifestyle has brought with it a fear of change. Many of us don't want to alter anything, be it a form of service, a stained-glass window, a musical setting, or a translation of the Bible. In an age of rapid and extreme change, change has become a bad word among many Christians. We seem to fear that only by holding on to the past will we be able to hold on to Christ. Convinced that the past belongs to him, we have doubt about the future, trembling that tomorrow may belong to somebody else. Indeed, the changes of recent years have been drastic and frequently destructive. One could say that those who are not shocked are simply insensitive. But if Christians know that God is at work in these changes also and "salvation is nearer to us now than when we first believed" they will say: "Behold, the dwelling of God is with men. He will dwell with them and they shall be his people, and God himself will be with them" (Rev. 21:3). This is the significance of hope.

As for the man who is weak in faith, welcome him, but not for disputes over opinions. One believes he may eat anything, while the weak man eats only vegetables. Let not him who eats despise him who abstains, and let not him who abstains pass judgment on him who eats; for God has welcomed him. Who are you to pass judgment on the servant of another? It is before his own master that he stands or falls. And he will be upheld, for the Master is able to make him stand.

Romans 14:1-4

12

The Varieties of Christian Commitment

The next time you are in church look around and note the kinds of people who attend on any given Sunday. They are old and young, rich and poor, sick and healthy, intelligent and not so intelligent, well adjusted and at odds with themselves and everybody else. If everybody is alike in your church something is drastically wrong, for the Christian fellowship consists of all kinds of people.

Because it was always so Paul wrote to the Romans: "If a man is weak in his faith you must accept him without attempting to settle doubtful points" (Rom. 14:1 NEB). Agreement on all points is not necessary for acceptance into the Christian fellowship, for the quest for unity does not demand unanimity. Paul does not mean that all opinions are equally true, for he certainly was no relativist, but rather that there is room inside the church for the weak as well as the strong, and that in this world the church is always something of a mixed bag.

One of the most dangerous trends in Christendom is the tendency for the church to become a group of like-minded people who must agree on everything. A long-standing pattern of denominationalism, with its possibility for everybody in case of disagreement to pick up his marbles, go home, and start his own denomination, has contributed a great deal to the glorification of uniformity in the church.

Different people choose to glorify different areas where they insist on total agreement. Some like the worship service to be always the same. They cannot tolerate any variation from the accustomed liturgy—or lack of liturgy. This includes the vestments the minister wears. They will threaten to leave the church if the minister should conduct the service differently or wear different attire. Still others insist on uniformity of religious experience. You have to be able to give the exact day and hour when you "found Jesus" or you are not a real Christian. A prescribed emotional experience is necessary for recognition as a Christian by these people.

Among others, liturgy and religious experience are not as important as complete agreement on a particular interpretation of the Scriptures. If you believe that the story of Jonah is like the parable of the Prodigal Son, an illustration of God's mercy and not an historical account about a particular man, they will read you out of their church, since they accept only those who submit to their approved rules of scriptural interpretation.

Apparently Paul had some trouble with people who thought that one could not be a Christian if one ate meat. In turn, the meat-eaters were irritated by the vegetarians and despised them. Paul said: "The man who eats must not hold in contempt the man who does not, and he who does not eat must not pass judgment on the one who does; for God has accepted him" (Rom. 14:3 NEB). While vegetarianism is hardly an issue in our churches (and even in Paul's time the real issue probably was the fact that almost all meat sold had first been consecrated to pagan deities) similar issues are still troubling Christians, and congregations can be divided into the "weak" and the "strong."

Indeed, the typical Christian congregation today consists of at least three kinds of members who can be characterized by a different type of Christian commitment. First there are those who are committed to Christianity as part of their cultural heritage. They are good citizens of Christian background, and for such people being a Christian is part of their identity as human beings. They may not go to church very often, but they generally get to a service on Easter Sunday, are married in church, have their children baptized, and want a minister officiating at family funerals, including their own.

Then there are those who will accept all the practices and performances dear to the first group, but who in addition see in Christianity the teaching of a way of life exemplary for themselves and desirable for everybody else. They want people to read the Bible because it is the "Good Book," and they want their children to attend church school and church because they approve and admire the moral teachings of Christianity. Even if they do not always practice what the church preaches, they have no doubt that the moral teachings of Christianity are true, and that they themselves would be happier if they were more faithful in following them.

The third group is different. Its representatives may accept all the practices of the former groups, but they know that they are Christians not because of their cultural tradition or moral practice but because Jesus Christ is their Lord and Savior. They know also that this meeting is not something they deserve, but rather a gift of God's grace which has surprised and overwhelmed them. They now are trying to find ways to express their gratitude for the love that has found them and will not let them go.

All three groups can be found in the typical Christian congregation—the cultural Christian, the moral Christian, and the overpowered Christian, the people caught up in Christ in such a way that they cannot help being what they are. They cannot take any credit for their state, for it is something which happened to them and which they do not fully understand.

The question is, how can these different varieties of Christians live together in harmony? Probably the third group is the "strongest," the second "weaker," and the first "weakest," to use Paul's terminology. Paul says to all of us, let each other be: "Who are you to pass judgement on someone else's servant? Whether he stands or falls is his own Master's business; and stand he will, because his Master has power to enable him to stand" (Rom. 14:4 NEB). The lesson is: Christians must not trust their own commitment but rather the Master who has made a variety of commitments possible.

One man esteems one day as better than another, while another man esteems all days alike. Let every one be fully convinced in his own mind. He who observes the day, observes it in honor of the Lord. He also who eats, eats in honor of the Lord, since he gives thanks to God; while he who abstains, abstains in honor of the Lord and gives thanks to God. None of us lives to himself, and none of us dies to himself. If we live, we live to the Lord, and if we die, we die to the Lord; so then, whether we live or whether we die, we are the Lord's. For to this end Christ died and lived again, that he might be Lord both of the dead and of the living.

Romans 14:5-9

13

The Source of Unity and Diversity

Since the early Christians came from a variety of social, racial, economic, and religious backgrounds, they brought a multitude of customs and ethnic traditions into their new life in the church. Most striking to Paul was the difference in the way Christians of Jewish background felt about the Sabbath as compared with Gentile Christians. He did not mind that these Jewish Christians faithfully kept the Sabbath in the manner practiced among the orthodox. But he insisted that Gentile Christians were free "to esteem all days alike."

This was not a trivial example of Paul's openness to diversity in the Christian movement, for he had been raised as an orthodox Jew himself and was aware of the central importance of Sabbath observance in his tradition. It is probable that he himself observed the Sabbath as customary among Jews. In questions of this sort he appealed to conscience. He wanted people to "be fully convinced in their own minds," and not to do things which might destroy their relationship to the Lord. He suggested to the Romans that those who felt that they honored the Lord by observing the Sabbath were free to do so. Those who felt that such observance might confuse their relationship to the Lord should not even consider it.

In the pluralistic world of the first century, and with Christians coming from every conceivable background, it was important to make distinctions between central and peripheral issues. Rules concerning food and the observance of holy days seemed peripheral to Paul.

The unity of the Christian movement was not based on such practices, but rather on the Christian's relationship to his Lord. "None of us lives to himself, and none of us dies to himself. If we live, we live to the Lord, and if we die, we die to the Lord; so then, whether we live or whether we die, we are the Lord's." This seemed to put the matter of diet and Sabbath observance in the proper perspective.

In later years, when Christianity had become the official religion of the state and eventually the established religion in most countries of Europe and America, it became more difficult to distinguish between ethnic traditions and the Christian gospel, and to many people their cultural heritage seemed more significant than the proclamation of Christ. Being a Roman Catholic became identified with being Irish or Italian, just as being Lutheran was identified with being Scandinavian or German, and being Presbyterian with a Scottish heritage. A by-product of this ethnic emphasis was that the language of worship, particularly in populations of mixed ethnic background, became ever more important as a mark of Christian distinctiveness. Latin was for Roman Catholics; German, the Scandinavian languages, and perhaps Slovak were Lutheran languages; and Anglo-Christians were supposed to use English.

It was an important development in the first half of the twentieth century that all Christians in America learned to speak English even in their worship; and since Vatican II it is difficult to find a Mass said in Latin among English-speaking worshipers.

Food and games also played an important role in Christian identification and diversity, and one used to be able to distinguish various denominations by the kind of supper they were giving to support their activities. The church of the lutefisk dinner or sauerkraut supper or bingo every Thursday was a more accurate and generally recognized description of denominations than any account of the theology taught in the various buildings.

The ecumenical movement was an important factor in the examination of the sources of unity and diversity among Christians. Some features of the Christian lifestyle as practiced by the various denominations were clearly "nontheological," the result of traditions only tenuously related to the faith. Other differences were more profound and reflected a different theological perspective.

If we now look at this situation in the light of Paul's exhortation to the Romans, what can we learn for our time? First of all, differences are not of themselves bad. Paul had said earlier that differences between individuals are useful for the church. "Having gifts that differ according to the grace given to us, let us use them" (Rom. 12:6). Here he asserts that there is room within the Christian movement for group differences. There is hardly a church today where there are not differences in taste among the members. Nowadays it is often not a preference in food but rather a difference in taste in music or style of worship. Paul seems to advocate considerable openness. The question he asks us is: "How do you honor the Lord best? How do you thank Him most appropriately?" He suggests: "Let every one be fully convinced in his own mind." It does not matter much how modern or old-fashioned our worship is, as long as it is genuinely ours. We may need a variety of forms to meet the genuine needs of a variety of people. There is nothing wrong with using a formal service for people who worship best in such a setting, and an informal service for those who are bored by formality. Such differences do not matter—they may even prove creative—but when they divide Christians from each other, we are in trouble.

We are seeing much that is new and exciting happening among Christians in our day. The question we must always ask is: "Who is being glorified?" Paul says, "None of us lives to himself, and none of us dies to himself." Do we honor human beings? Do we celebrate *our* profound religious experience? Do we hallow *our* loyalty to the Bible? Do we congratulate ourselves on *our* moral superiority to other Christians? If we revel in our own superiority, for whatever reason, our differences are evil and destructive, and our unity is built on sand. If we use our differences to give glory to the Lord they will contribute to the richness of our unity. The source of our diversity is God's creative richness, which has made us able to praise him in many ways; the source of our unity is the Lord. In him we are always one—in spite of our diversities.

Why do you pass judgment on your brother?
Or you, why do you despise your brother? For
we shall all stand before the judgment seat of
God; for it is written, "As I live, says the Lord,
every knee shall bow to me, and every tongue
shall give praise to God." So each of us shall
give account of himself to God.

Romans 14:10-12

14

The Importance of Perspective

One of the difficulties small children have in understanding the world around them comes from their lack of perspective. For a baby, the mother's departure for a quick shopping trip is of equal significance with her departure for a month's stay in the hospital. Tomorrow, next year, or ten years from now are all the same to a small child because he has no perspective on time.

Occasionally a scientist writes an article about the change of climate that we can anticipate on this earth. He may predict a new ice age or a steady increase in the temperature of the earth which will melt the ice caps and drown millions. It makes a difference to us whether he talks about something that may happen next year, a hundred years from now, or in ten thousand years. Our perspective changes if it involves most of us (next year), none of us (a hundred years from now), or an age we cannot even imagine (ten thousand years hence).

When Paul writes about the matter of judging or despising people he tries to put the subject into the proper Christian perspective by reminding us that "we shall all stand before the judgment seat of God." He believes that if we keep this fact in mind our tendency to look down on other people or look up to them as almost superhuman will disappear and we will be able to see our position in proper perspective.

How many conflicts in a home could be avoided or at least reduced in significance if we were to remember Paul's counsel? Parents who judge their children harshly because of differences in lifestyle should ask themselves, How will this argument about clothing or hair or even the messy room look when "we shall stand before the judgment seat of God?" Children who despise their parents for their taste in music or their ignorance of current fashions should ask themselves, What will be my attitude when "we shall stand before the judgment seat of God?" Most family arguments vanish into insignificance if we approach them with the perspective Paul suggests.

But how about the arguments at work? How will my envy, caused by a promotion somebody else received, look before God's judgment seat? How will my claim to be smarter, more efficient, and better in my job than all my fellow workers look from that point of view? Even in our national life, how important will the most exalted leader of our nation look before that judgment seat—what privileges will he be able to claim then? How will the righteousness of those politicians who have not recently been caught look on that day?

In short, what Paul does is to relativize the standards of judgment we use on each other by putting them into proper perspective and holding them up against the judgment of God. The result for Christians should be that we look with suspicion on all human claims of superiority and question any effort to dehumanize certain people who do not measure up to our standards. The American Declaration of Independence eloquently disavowed such dehumanization. When Jefferson wanted to establish the equality of all human beings, he brought God, the Creator, into the political discussion and said, "All men are created equal." From this perspective the differences between human beings vanished. Before God, we are equal.

Christians have an obligation in our time to point out the penultimate character of all human judgments in the light of God's judgment. What is the basis of judgment on our brothers and sisters? Whom do we exclude from our society because we despise them? A common device is money. We do not like to see poor people, partly because they make us feel guilty for not helping them, partly because we claim that their poverty is self-inflicted; they deserve their poverty, as we deserve our affluence. We devise elaborate schemes to explain how our hard work has made us what we are, while their sloth has brought ruin upon them. What have we done to deserve being born in a state of affluence? What has the baby dying from starvation in sub-Saharan Africa done to deserve its fate? Our hypocrisy is obvious and will not stand before the judgment seat of God.

Or we may use intelligence as a device to despise others. We have developed complex tests which purport to measure people's intelligence, and then those with high scores despise those with low scores. But before the judgment seat of God our highest score is unimpressive, and we are forced to listen with Job when God says to us: "Where were you when I laid the foundation of the earth? Tell me, if you have understanding. Who determined its measurements—surely you know! Or who stretched the line upon it? On what were its bases sunk, or who laid its cornerstone, when the morning stars sang together, and all the sons of God shouted for joy?" (Job 38:4-7).

One of the most foolish devices for judging others is race. One must be desperate if one has to depend on the pigmentation or lack of pigmentation in one's skin to pass judgment on people and despise them. Yet racism is pervasive and has brought incredible suffering to millions of people all over the world. Even religion has been used to despise and destroy people. Sometimes Christians have resorted to a pretended loyalty to God to justify passing judgment on those who do not share their beliefs. Even in our day religious wars are raging in some places in the world, and religious prejudice is not uncommon in the most liberal and democratic societies.

Paul, by reminding us of the fact that we shall stand before the judgment seat of God, places our life in perspective and recalls to us Jesus' words: "Judge not, that you be not judged. For with the judgment you pronounce you will be judged, and the measure you give will be the measure you get" (Matt. 7:1-2).

Then let us no more pass judgment on one another, but rather decide never to put a stumbling-block or hindrance in the way of a brother. I know and am persuaded in the Lord Jesus that nothing is unclean in itself; but it is unclean for any one who thinks it unclean. If your brother is being injured by what you eat, you are no longer walking in love. Do not let what you eat cause the ruin of one for whom Christ died. So do not let what is good to you be spoken of as evil.

Romans 14:13-16

15

Noblesse Oblige

Noblesse oblige. This French phrase suggests that those who have received high privileges are obligated to demonstrate generosity in their behavior toward those who have been less liberally endowed. It is the apostle Paul's recommendation for mature Christians as they deal with matters which are in themselves of little consequence but may mean a lot to those less mature in their faith. German parents tell their older children to be nice to their younger brothers and sisters with the exhortation *"Der Klügere gibt nach!"* ("the one who is more intelligent yields"). It is good advice and hard to follow. We want to show our superiority, we want our *noblesse* to be acknowledged, our intelligence to win points.

Paul proposes that precisely those Christians who know "not what goes into the mouth defiles a man, but what comes out of the mouth" (Matt. 15:11) ought to be willing to yield to those perturbed about food and drink. The obvious application to our present situation is the recurrent controversy about alcoholic beverages. If it offends a fellow Christian with whom I have a meal that I drink a glass of beer with my steak, I should probably forego the pleasure in order not to offend him. But where do we draw the line? Should I avoid beer even when my friend is not with me? Should I hide the bottles when he comes to visit me? Isn't Paul's exhortation an invitation to hypocrisy?

And what about the more serious matters? Should I go around claiming that the world was created in six twenty-four hour days or that the hare chews his cud (Lev. 11:6) because some of my fellow Christians are obsessed with what I consider an immature literalism? What about racism? Should I give in to the weaker brother who happens to believe in the superiority of the white race merely because he is ignorant or stupid and I should not put up a stumbling block? "The one who is more intelligent yields?"

Paul does not intend to teach hypocrisy. He wants us to act lovingly and to consider the true interests of the other person. Knowingly to offer an alcoholic a drink is certainly sinful. To have a glass of sherry in front of your Aunt Agnes, who is the local chairperson of the Women's Christian Temperance Union, is tactless. To make the Christian witness a proclamation of evolution rather than the Cross is false teaching, but to accept evolution as a plausible scientific explanation of the development of the species is an option open to Christian and non-Christian alike.

What Paul is suggesting is that we act lovingly towards each other and not use our greater insight, our deeper knowledge, to do violence to people who may know less. One of the greatest theological teachers in this century was Paul Tillich. An internationally respected authority on theology, he had the gift to entertain questions in such a manner that even a naive question, once he had reworded it, sounded useful and even profound. He used his vast knowledge to deepen questions and answer them, so that the questioner and the entire audience were led to a better understanding of the subject of the discussion.

Paul tells us in Romans 14:13-16 that we should always keep the interest of our fellow Christians in mind. In a discussion are we trying to score points or help our friend to understand the issue? Do we want to look good or do we want him to gain insight? Often the two concerns cannot be reconciled. We either win a friend or an argument. What is more important? This is not a trivial question, since it is a key to the outreach of the Christian church—to evangelism and mission. Are we motivated in our dealings with other people by the generosity which God has shown to us? Do we want to share the gifts we have received with them? Or are we motivated by the desire to be proven right and the ambition to prove our superiority?

In many discussions about religion, one has the impression that the participants are more concerned with demonstrating how right they are than with helping the other person with his problems. Does the eager propagandist who puts his foot into the door of your home to force his message upon you want to help you, gain points with his god, or prove himself religiously superior? Why is so much religious discussion a disparagement of the faith of the other person? Paul says, "let us no more pass judgment on one another," yet popular religious debate is very often precisely that—passing judgment upon one another. This applies not only to the debates among members of different major religious traditions but also to casual discussions between members of different congregations. Again and again we criticize and denigrate people without adequate information to substantiate our preconceived notions.

Noblesse oblige! In the light of what God has done for us, how can we be intolerant of our neighbor—even if he seems strange and obnoxious? We pray, "Forgive us our trespasses, as we forgive those who trespass against us," and are reminded of the story in Matthew 18:23-35 where Jesus tells about a servant who was forgiven a debt of ten thousand talents (according to the RSV, about ten million dollars) because he was bankrupt, and who then started choking a fellow servant who could not pay him the 100 denarii (about twenty dollars) which he owed him.

In view of the generosity with which God has treated us, the lifestyle of Christians should reflect the same generosity in our dealings with other men and women, particularly in an age where people are forced to live and work close together and have little opportunity to escape the pressure of the crowd by going to the desert. The advice of Paul is practical and valuable: "Then let us no more pass judgment on one another, but rather decide never to put a stumbling block or hindrance in the way of a brother"— especially if he is a little hard to take!

For the kingdom of God does not mean food and drink but righteousness and peace and joy in the Holy Spirit; he who thus serves Christ is acceptable to God and approved by men. Let us then pursue what makes for peace and for mutual upbuilding.

Romans 14:17-19

16

Signs of the Kingdom

We are familiar with ethnic stereotypes. People tend to attribute particular characteristics to various nationalities. Scots are supposed to be tightfisted, the French great lovers, the Irish eloquent. These stereotypes are the basis of the ethnic joke and are reflected in the familiar story about the Englishman, the German, the Frenchman, the American, and the Norwegian who were supposed to write a story on the elephant. The Englishman wrote an essay, "The Elephant and the Empire." The German wrote a three-volume work, "Prolegomena to Any Future Study of the Elephant." The Frenchman wrote "The Love-Life of the Elephant." The American wrote "Why American Zoos Have Bigger and Better Elephants." The Norwegian wrote a monograph, "Norway and Norwegians."

In Romans 14:17-19 Paul tries to establish the Christian stereotype, the character of the typical citizen of God's kingdom, and asserts that the signs of the kingdom are righteousness, peace, and joy. The Christian is recognized by the fact that he shares in God's righteousness now and forever, that he has God's peace now and always, and that he can rejoice now and eternally. "For the kingdom of God does not mean food and drink but righteousness and peace and joy in the Holy Spirit."

In the context of this letter Paul is saying to the strong Christians: "Don't get excited about diets; even if your brother would eat and drink without fear, as you do, it would not really matter. What matters is that you and he share in the righteousness and the peace and the joy which we have in the Holy Spirit." But here it becomes apparent that the signs of the kingdom Paul talks about are not like the ethnic stereotypes mentioned earlier. For the righteousness and the peace and the joy are not really possessions of the Christian. They are not his or her characteristics. Christians bear these marks in a hidden and obscure way. They will possess them fully only in the coming kingdom of God.

Paul says we are just or righteous because God has declared us just or righteous for Christ's sake. But we all know at the same time how deeply we are still involved in injustice. For example, I may be a teacher, and it is a part of my job to give grades to my students. These grades, hard as I may try to be fair, are never as just as I would like them to be. As a teacher I am just and unjust at the same time. Or I may be a parent. I want to be as impartial as possible in the treatment of my children, but I never have all the facts. One of my children is more clever in manipulating me than any of the others, and thus I treat her as a favorite. Again I am just and unjust at the same time.

In business, in government, at work and at play, wherever we are we experience the problem of our righteousness. In Luther's phrase, we learn that we are righteous and sinners at the same time, that our righteousness is but a foretaste and intimation of God's realm of righteousness which is coming towards us. Righteousness is not a Christian stereotype, but a precious and precarious gift.

And the same is true about "peace." It, too, is a gift which God gives to his people. As Jesus says in the Gospel of John, "Peace I leave with you; my peace I give to you" (John 14:27). But in this world we always have this peace ambiguously. In the coming kingdom of God there will be no kind of sickness, evil, or discord. In this world we are all under constant pressure, suffering all manner of ills, especially the sickness unto death, assaulted by evil on every side, and at odds with God, our neighbor, and ourselves. We get glimpses of this peace, but when we try to settle in peace we realize that people cry, "Peace, Peace," and there is no peace. Again, peace is not a Christian stereotype but a promise which we possess in hope.

And what about joy? Jesus said, "In the world you have tribulation" (John 16:33). This "tribulation," this anxiety, is the exact opposite of joy and every Christian is only too aware of this pressure which surrounds him, even though he may indeed be a child of God. He can rejoice in spite of the anxiety, for joy is not a psychological achievement but a spiritual gift. We are Christians not because we always keep smiling (this is the silly stereotype), but because we know that even when we are sad or afraid or anxious God is willing to give us his joy now and in the future. Thus the joy we experience now occasionally is a down payment on the joy of the children of God in the coming kingdom of God. Here we still sing with William Cowper:

> Where is the blessedness I knew
>> When first I saw the Lord?
> Where is the soul-refreshing view
>> Of Jesus and his word?
>
> What peaceful hours I once enjoyed!
>> How sweet their memory still!
> But they have left an aching void
>> The world can never fill.

> (*Service Book and Hymnal*, hymn 466)

Thus, Paul's signs of the kingdom—righteousness, peace, and joy—are real, but they are quite different from the ethnic stereotypes to which we are accustomed. The signs of the kingdom are just that, *signs* which point towards the future. Indeed, we share in them now, but we hold them loosely and partially and tentatively. We are not citizens of God's kingdom because of our own righteousness, but rather because Christ's righteousness covers our unrighteousness. We are not citizens of the kingdom of God because of the peace we possess now. We have little peace of our own, but God is always willing to give us his peace which overcomes our own contentiousness and aggression. And we are not citizens of the kingdom of God because of the joy we have attained but because of the joy we anticipate at the end of our pilgrimage towards the kingdom whose citizens we are now even while we are living in exile. The signs of the kingdom are not the religious stereotypes of the Christian; they inspire and encourage us on our pilgrimage to the just, peaceable, and joyful kingdom!

Do not, for the sake of food, destroy the work of God. Everything is indeed clean, but it is wrong for any one to make others fall by what he eats; it is right not to eat meat or drink wine or do anything that makes your brother stumble. The faith that you have, keep between yourself and God; happy is he who has no reason to judge himself for what he approves. But he who has doubts is condemned, if he eats, because he does not act from faith; for whatever does not proceed from faith is sin.
Romans 14:20-23

17

The Nature of Sin

Most people if asked to name the opposite of "sin" would probably say "virtue." We speak of seven cardinal virtues in contrast to the seven deadly sins, and believe that we are able to identify the sinner through the sinful acts he performs. For Paul the opposite of sin is faith. "For whatever does not proceed from faith is sin."

If we look more closely we can see that sin has two dimensions: psychologically it is pride, theologically it is unbelief. Pride is the basic human expression of unbelief. It was the tragic flaw that was the subject of Greek drama. It was his *hybris*, his pride, which destroyed the Greek hero, who is not so much an evil person, in the sense that he intends to do evil deeds, as a person who thinks that he has all the answers and as a result produces disaster for himself and all those about him. Thus J. Robert Oppenheimer, the noted physicist who was in charge of the development of the atom bomb, spoke of sin as pride when he said in a lecture: "In some crude sense which no vulgarity, no humor, no overstatement can quite extinguish, the physicists have known sin; and this is a knowledge which they cannot lose." He thought of sin here as pride—the pride in their own righteousness which allowed scientists to design and produce instruments of mass destruction and then assist in their deadly use.

This is one of the two profound aspects of sin, the pride that makes us believe that we have all the answers and that we human beings are "gods" which the allegedly mindless and godless evolutionary process has produced. Therefore life and death, good and evil, truth and falsehood are ours to determine. We can decide who should live and who should die, what is right and what is wrong, what is real and what is not. As we look around us we see everywhere the results of this human pride as it affects us from birth to death. We decide who is to be born and which fetus is to become the object of medical experimentation. We decide what behavior is to be positively reinforced and what behavior is to be curtailed. We decide what truth is useful for people to hear and what truth is only for the ears of censors and certain select politicians. We decide whose opinions may be presented at a public meeting and who should be shouted down before he can be heard. We decide who may live and who must die, who will get the use of the kidney machine and who will not, who will be the donor of a heart transplant and who will be the recipient. And all this is done under the heading "I can do no wrong, because my heart is pure." Nobody is unaffected by this pride. This is why Christians claim that sin is pervasive and that all human beings are sinners.

But, besides this psychological dimension of sin as pride, sin has also a theological dimension, and here we can describe it as unbelief. It is because we do not fear and love and trust God above all things that we are full of pride and are sinners. Luther believed that all Ten Commandments were implicit in the First Commandment, "I am the Lord thy God; thou shalt have no other gods before me." Every act which people call "sin" is a result of having other gods; it is a symptom of unbelief. Why does a person lie? Because he wants to impress somebody, because he wants to shirk responsibility, because he wants to get himself out of trouble. Because he fears, loves, and trusts somebody or something else more than God. Any evil thought, word, or deed is the result of trouble in our relationship with God. If we loved God above all things, these thoughts would not arise, these words would not be spoken, these deeds would not be done.

Luther saw that coveting, stealing, bearing false witness, adultery, murder, neglect of parents (not to mention direct offenses against God) were caused by the broken relationship between human beings and God, from unbelief. Similarly Augustine, the great African theologian, claimed that if you really loved God you could do what you pleased, because you would naturally do what pleases God.

Our problem is that we do what may please masters that are

not God, and especially that we do what pleases us. This explains another descriptive phrase for sin in the Christian vocabulary, "to be turned into yourself." The sinner is the person who cares only about himself or about *his* family, *his* job, *his* country, *his* car, *his* golf game. The false gods may be quite impressive, like family or country, or utterly trivial, like a car or golf game, but they have one thing in common: they turn us away from God and into ourselves.

Because of the variety of our loyalties, we may easily confuse sin and crime. A crime is the breaking of a human law, a rule human beings have established for the maintenance of their society. Sin is always the result of our trouble with God. Something can be a sin and not a crime. For example, thoughts can be sinful but never criminal. Something can be both a sin and a crime, such as murder. Something may be a crime but not a sin. When the early Christians refused to sacrifice to the genius of the Roman emperor they committed a crime but they did not sin. We have seen similar situations in our time when people have broken unjust laws which enforced the segregation of races, or refused to serve in a war which their consciences told them was unjust and against God's will.

Sin as pride and sin as unbelief are pervasive. As Paul has said earlier in his letter to the Romans, we are Christians not because we are free from sin but because Christ died for our sins. The Christian lifestyle results from the forgiveness of Christ, not from our human virtue and perfections.

*We who are strong ought to bear with the
failings of the weak, and not to please ourselves;
let each of us please his neighbor for his good,
to edify him. For Christ did not please himself;
but, as it is written, "The reproaches of those
who reproached thee fell on me."*

Romans 15:1-3

18

The Model

In one of the greatest paintings in the Christian tradition, Grünewald's Isenheim altar, we see a pain-racked Jesus hanging on a cross and John the Baptist standing on the side pointing to direct the attention of the viewer to Jesus. The final argument in all discussions among Christians is always Jesus, the Christ. Without him all Christian speech is empty talk. With him in the picture everything begins to make sense. This is as true about ethics as it is about theology. Thus, when Paul wants to clinch his arguments about the responsibility of the strong for the weak within the Christian community he simply points to Christ: "For Christ did not please himself; but, as it is written, 'the reproaches of those who reproached thee fell on me.'"

Jesus is the outstanding example of the strong bearing the failings of the weak. As Paul wrote in Philippians 2:5-8: "Have this mind among yourselves, which you have in Christ Jesus, who, though he was in the form of God, did not count equality with God a thing to be grasped, but emptied himself, taking the form of a servant, being born in the likeness of men. And being found in human form he humbled himself and became obedient unto death, even death on a cross."

In dealing with what Paul calls the "weaker" fellow Christians and other people seeking meaning in their life, Paul suggests that we use Jesus as our model. This involves two acts: identification and proclamation. These two at first seem hard to reconcile. It is possible to identify so completely with the weak as to become as weak as they are. The story is told about the policeman who was such an expert in dealing with potential suicides that he would always be sent to the bridge to talk the would-be suicide out of his desperate leap. He did a good job because he was able to identify with the people. One day, the story goes, a man who wanted to jump described his disgust with life and its meaninglessness so persuasively that he talked the policeman into jumping with him. This is identification without proclamation.

The opposite problem develops when the Christian believer describes his faith, without reference to any periods of doubt or questioning, in such glowing terms that the listener is simply unable to relate to such certainty. It strikes him as overconfidence and opinionatedness. Thus Miguel de Unamuno, one of the wisest observers of our age, could say, "Faith which does not doubt is dead faith." People who approach those they want to help with such overwhelming assurance tend to destroy all possibility for communication and produce the reaction in their listener, "Methinks she does protest too much." This was the problem with the generally well-intentioned efforts of the "Jesus-people," whose dogmatism could not penetrate a doubting age. When you have no real link with the people you are trying to guide, your efforts become bizarre demonstrations of behavior which is simply incomprehensible to the people you are trying to influence. This is one of the most important problems any missionary here or abroad has to face and solve.

For this reason Paul points us to Jesus. He identified with us by being born, maturing, eating, drinking, rejoicing and weeping, agonizing and dying, as one of us. This is, of course, the great identification, the incarnation which makes Jesus our man and our model. Jesus carried this identification into the small details of life. He apparently could go without food for extended periods of time—but he fed the hungry nevertheless, identifying with their weakness. He fed them and healed them and spoke to them about the coming kingdom of God. He proclaimed the gospel.

Jesus saved the woman taken in adultery from a mob and told her, "Go, and do not sin again" (John 8:11). With Jesus it is always identification and proclamation. But the relationship of the two is one of the great dilemmas facing the Christian church in our time. We have those who advocate identification. Go to the hungry and oppressed and support them in their struggle for a better life and freedom. Use the resources of the church to build a better world. Too long has the church dispensed the

Christian faith as an opiate for the people, killing the painful symptoms of their sickness and not dealing with the underlying causes. We have no right to proclaim anything to anybody, they shout; we must aid the revolutionaries without asking questions because our failures of the past have abolished our right to speak; we may only listen.

On the other side there are those who do not want to identify with anybody until he has accepted our point of view and joined our church. They want to help only those who are "of the household of faith" and make sure that their aid goes only to those people with whom they agree or who at least will first listen to their speeches. Like the Midnight Missions in the slum districts of some of our cities, they have the sandwiches in the window of their storefront mission and the hot coffee ready for those who are willing to sing some hymns and sit through a prayer meeting.

Jesus identified with all people, even those who were to demand his crucifixion a little later. He spoke to them, too, but his help did not depend on their first signing on the dotted line. The Christian lifestyle demands identification and proclamation. But the proclamation will only be understood if the identification has been genuine. Jesus was what he said; Christians must become what they proclaim.

For whatever was written in former days was written for our instruction, that by steadfastness and by the encouragement of the scriptures we might have hope. May the God of steadfastness and encouragement grant you to live in such harmony with one another, in accord with Christ Jesus, that together you may with one voice glorify the God and Father of our Lord Jesus Christ.

Romans 15:4-6

19

The Function of the Scriptures

One of the most serious problems modern people have as they try to come to terms with the Christian faith is understanding the authority of the Scriptures among Christians. They know that there are many holy books revered by people all over the world. Hindus and Buddhists, Confucians and Taoists have their sacred writings. Why do Christians insist on the importance of the Bible, these particular sixty-six books that come to us from Palestine?

What is the function of the Scriptures in the Christian life? This was not much of an issue for Christians of Jewish background. They read the Bible as the exciting and encouraging history of their people. The stories about Moses, Saul, and David were to them as the stories about our nation's greatest leaders are to us. But the Gentile Christians in Rome and most of us today cannot make this "ethnic" identification with the Old Testament stories. This led some people, for example, the followers of a shipbuilder by the name of Marcion, very soon to discard the Old Testament and to select as their Bible only those parts of the New Testament that were not "tainted" with the Jewish story. Paul insists, however, that the whole Bible (and for him this is in effect the Old Testament, since he was just then writing what became eventually part of the New Testament) is essential for the Christian life. He says that the Bible "was written for our instruction, that by steadfastness and by the encouragement of the scriptures we might have hope."

For Paul the Scriptures instruct us to be steadfast and to have hope. If you ask, "Why?" the answer is that they show us that God has been faithful to his people and kept his promise by sending Jesus, the Christ, who is his son and our savior. Or as the author of the letter to the Hebrews put it: "In many and various ways God spoke of old to our fathers by the prophets. But in these last days he has spoken to us by a son" (Heb. 1:1-2). It is through the message of the Bible that we are enabled to "live in such harmony with one another, in accord with Christ Jesus, that together [we] may with one voice glorify the God and Father of our Lord Jesus Christ."

For Paul the Bible is unique and authoritative because it brings us to Christ. Everything else is unimportant. Other sacred books may have sound moral advice or tell beautiful stories about the creation of the world. The discussion between Lord Krishna and Arjuna about the duty of the soldier told in the *Bhagavad-Gita* may rightly move us to tears. *The Life of Buddha* is a poignant tale of human courage and compassion. But only the Bible tells us about Jesus who is the Christ. The foundation of the Bible is to keep Christ always before the Christian. The Christian studies the Bible to be reminded of God's plan for mankind which is accomplished through Jesus, the Christ. And Paul insists that if this is done it will result in steadfastness, encouragement, hope, and harmony. Steadfastness is a matter of orientation, of having something to hold on to. The British historian Herbert Butter-field wrote in his book *Christianity and History*: "Hold on to Christ and for the rest be totally uncommitted." This is the steadfastness of the ballet dancer who can turn rapidly and not become dizzy because he has his eyes fixed at one point, however fast he may turn. Paul says the Christian must be so oriented towards Christ Jesus that nothing can distract or confuse him. It is in the Scriptures that Christ meets him and enables him to be steadfast. And when this has happened the experiences of the many people encountered in the Scriptures encourage him to remain steadfast and to have hope.

The Christian reads the Bible not merely as history but as the symbol of God's dealing with human beings. He identifies with Adam and Eve, Abraham and Sarah, Deborah and David, Peter, Mary Magdalene, and Thomas. These are all people in whose experience he participates and who encourage him to hope against hope and to expect Christ to be faithful even if men deny him as Peter did or doubt him like Thomas.

Martin Luther wrote once, "That is the true test by which to judge all books, when we see whether or not they inculcate

Christ [*Christum treiben*]. For all the Scriptures show us Christ" (*Preface to the Epistles of St. James and St. Jude*). The function of the Scriptures is to confront us with Christ. Luther had learned this from Paul, for whom everything depends on being "in accord with Christ Jesus." Scripture does many other things as well. It tells the story of a people, it presents a mighty and poetic vision of the beginning and the end of the world. It gives all kinds of sound advice, but the center is Christ, and when that is lost sight of the rest cannot save anybody.

The function of the Scriptures is to keep Christ before us and to keep us oriented in the rapid and drastic changes in our time. Other people at other times might have been able to do without such a center to their life. In more stable ages such a point of orientation may have seemed less urgent, since changes came slowly and the world which one left at death was not significantly different from the world into which one was born. It is precisely because of the turbulent world in which we live that Christians can pray with Paul, who lived in an equally confused time, "May the God of steadfastness and encouragement grant us to live in such harmony with one another, in accord with Christ Jesus, that together we may with one voice glorify the God and Father of our Lord Jesus Christ."

Welcome one another, therefore, as Christ has welcomed you, for the glory of God. For I tell you that Christ became a servant to the circumcised to show God's truthfulness, in order to confirm the promises given to the patriarchs, and in order that the Gentiles might glorify God for his mercy. As it is written, "Therefore I will praise thee among the Gentiles, and sing to thy name"; and again it is said, "Rejoice, O Gentiles, with his people"; and again, "Praise the Lord, all Gentiles, and let all the peoples praise him"; and further Isaiah says, "The root of Jesse shall come, he who rises to rule the Gentiles; in him shall the Gentiles hope." May the God of hope fill you with all joy and peace in believing, so that by the power of the Holy Spirit you may abound in hope.

Romans 15:7-13

20

The Savior of the Gentiles

There was a time, before legislation made such practices illegal, when certain hotels and restaurants used to display signs which proclaimed "Gentiles Only." Paul ends his letter to the mixed group of Roman Christians of Jewish and Gentile background by proclaiming "Gentiles Also." In view of the overwhelming and inexhaustible grace that we all have received we must "welcome one another, as Christ has welcomed you, for the glory of God." Or, as the New English Bible translates this passage: "In a word, accept one another as Christ accepted us." As you live your life remember that Christ has welcomed you—regardless of your background. He is not interested in where you came from, but he cares where you are going. It is this conviction of the early Christians that God is no respecter of persons, that he poured out his grace on all humankind, which gives Christianity its unique power.

Why did the Christian movement win the support of the Hellenistic world in a short three hundred years? It is apparent that these Christians had little going for them as human beings measure reasons for success. Paul wrote quite openly to the Corinthians: "My brothers, think what sort of people you are, whom God has called. Few of you are men of wisdom, by any human standard; few are powerful or highly born" (1 Cor. 1:26 NEB). What was the reason for their success? The Jewish background of their leaders was no asset, for Juvenal and Martial, Roman authors of the time, reveal pervasive anti-Jewish feelings among leaders and common people in the Roman Empire. It certainly was not their superior organizational skill. If we can trust the epistles, our Communion services are better organized than the Communion services in Corinth. At least we don't have some members get drunk while others get only water. And however much our benevolence record may leave to be desired, we don't send missionaries to far-off places to collect contributions for the saints in our biggest city. But you recall that the church in Jerusalem did just that, and this was apparently one reason Paul got his position as Apostle to the Gentiles; headquarters in Jerusalem thought that he might bring in some money!

It was not the rhetorical skill of the apostles either. If the sermons of the Acts of the Apostles are an illustration, the preachers had a tendency to repeat themselves and they certainly were neither brilliant nor funny. Luke tells us that Paul's preaching put a young man by the name of Eutychus to sleep so that he fell out of a third story window (Acts 20:9).

But in spite of all these shortcomings, a mass movement developed which was so large and powerful by 325 A.D. that the emperor Constantine considered becoming a Christian the best way to obtain a power base that would enable him to rule. What was the secret of the Christian success? It is revealed in this verse: "Accept each other as Christ accepted us!" The amazing openness of the Christians towards all people was their secret weapon. One must listen to a Greek philosopher of the time in order to appreciate how this openness struck the contemporary world. In his anti-Christian propaganda book the philosopher Celsus described the Christian approaches to the Gentile world in these words:

> Let no one come to us who has been instructed or who is wise or prudent (for such qualifications are deemed evil by us); but if there be any ignorant or unintelligent or uninstructed or foolish persons, let them come with confidence.

And Celsus disdainfully continued:

> By which words acknowledging that such individuals are worthy of their God, they manifestly show that they desire and are able to gain over only the silly and the mean and the stupid, with women and children.

Granted that Celsus put the most negative interpretation possible on the well-known attitude of his Christian opponents, it is apparent that their open invitation to all kinds and conditions of men struck him as peculiar, mean, and perverse. "Indeed," he added, "what other person would a robber summon to himself by proclamation."

This is how the outside world understood Paul's exhortation: "Accept one another as Christ accepted us!" The success of Christianity resulted from its destruction of all conventional barriers to the acceptance of human beings into fellowship. Everybody is invited. Since Jesus died for the ungodly, the new life is open to all human beings. Jesus is the savior of the Gentiles. But "Gentiles" means here all those who know themselves to be rejected. People may consider themselves "Gentiles" in this negative sense for many reasons. They may not think they are clever enough to understand the true religion; it doesn't matter, they are accepted. They may think women are unwelcome. In Paul's experience it took ten men to worship; ten or even a hundred women would not do. All this was changed. The first Christian church in Europe met at the home of a business-woman in Philippi. They may not think they have the right race—but Ethiopian Gentiles are welcome, such as the treasurer of Candace, the queen of Ethiopia (Acts 8:27). Later Irenaeus will say barbarians are welcome. They may not be able to handle the Greek language elegantly, but they are accepted nevertheless.

One could be an outcast for many reasons. I may be rejected by my enemies and become a Gentile, a barbarian, a gook, a nonperson; that is bad! I may be rejected by my friends and become an outcast; and that is worse! I may be rejected by myself and consider myself an outcast, a nonperson, and that is the worst thing that can happen to me. Paul knew, because it had happened to him, and therefore he proclaims the gospel with such fervor: Christ has accepted us, though we are not acceptable. "Praise the Lord, all Gentiles, and let all the peoples praise him."

I myself am satisfied about you, my brethren,
that you yourselves are full of goodness, filled
with all knowledge, and able to instruct one
another. But on some points I have written to
you very boldly by way of reminder, because of
the grace given me by God to be a minister of
Christ Jesus to the Gentiles in the priestly
service of the gospel of God, so that the offering
of the Gentiles may be acceptable, sanctified
by the Holy Spirit. In Christ Jesus, then, I have
reason to be proud of my work for God. For
I will not venture to speak of anything except
what Christ has wrought through me to win
obedience from the Gentiles, by word and
deed, by the power of signs and wonders, by
the power of the Holy Spirit, so that from
Jerusalem and as far round as Illyricum I have
fully preached the gospel of Christ, thus making
it my ambition to preach the gospel, not where
Christ has already been named, lest I build on
another man's foundation, but as it is written,
"They shall see who have never been told of
him, and they shall understand who have
never heard of him."

Romans 15:14-21

21

Accepting Our Acceptance

It is hard to help people you don't really like. Somehow they sense how you feel about them and tend to pay little attention to anything you say or do. Effective communication cannot be based on contempt; it must be built on respect. This is as true for the relationship of nations as it is for the relationship in families. People who know that you despise them are not going to listen to you. One of the great gifts of Paul was his ability to like people. This positive attitude came through even when, as in his first letter to the Corinthians, he had to reprimand his audience severely. A person who writes to you, "I give thanks to God always for you," can get away with a lot of criticizing later.

In his letter to the Romans he concluded by calling the Roman Christians "full of goodness, filled with all knowledge, and able to instruct one another." He accepted the Romans as committed and worthwhile people. As a result, he had a good chance to be taken seriously by them. In that approach he is quite different from those Christians who get their satisfaction out of observing how evil and stupid everybody else is. The unpopularity of many so-called Christians is the direct result of the fact that they exude an overpowering sense of superiority which makes it difficult for ordinary mortals to listen to them.

Why was Paul able to accept the Christians in Rome so easily and openly? The answer becomes clear when we notice how he feels about himself. "In Christ Jesus, then, I have reason to be proud of my work for God." Paul's secret is that he knows that God has accepted him because he has experienced the love and power of Christ. Because God has accepted him he can accept himself, and because he can accept himself he can accept the people in Rome, Corinth, and Philippi—the entire world of Jews and Gentiles, women and men, free and slaves. We observe a chain reaction which starts with God and ends with the neighbor. If you can accept the fact that God loves you, you are able to accept yourself and other people.

Sometimes Christians think that they demonstrate their faith by describing in great detail what miserable sinners they used to be. You can usually get a crowd together if you promise them that some criminal, a murderer or rapist, will testify about his conversion. People love to hear such stories because the brightness of the Christian life is shown most splendidly against the somber background of a spectacularly sinful past. Unfortunately, the presentation usually gets mired down in the lurid description of the past. Little is said about the new life that Christ has made possible.

Paul is more interested in the future than in the past, in where we are going than where we came from. God accepted Paul unconditionally, while he was persecuting Christians and on the way to Damascus to extend his anti-Christian activities. Christ met him, and accepted him. But that wasn't the end of the story. From that day on, Christ worked through him and he could say, "from Jerusalem and as far round as Illyricum I have fully preached the gospel of Christ." The person who has accepted his acceptance is free for the future. Paul's ministry is a spectacular example of what this can mean. While he sometimes referred to his days as a persecutor of Christians, his emphasis was always on the new life of service which God had made possible for him, and he gave thanks that he had been allowed to work harder as a servant of Christ than anybody else.

The Christian lifestyle is not obsessed by the past but is directed towards the future. It is determined by hope, which for Paul belongs together with faith and love. Paul illustrates how acceptance becomes the basis for a life of service. He says it produced in him the "ambition to preach the gospel." Obsession with the past tends to be paralyzing. This is why Carl Sandburg could say, "I tell you the past is a bucket of ashes." Christians are freed for today, and they know that the future belongs to their Lord. And as they are freed from the burden of the past they are also freed from the attempts to save themselves by making themselves acceptable in the eyes of God. Once a person is aware of God's love he can devote his time to the interests of his neighbor without regard to the attention or gratitude which such acts may evoke. As long as we believe that our acceptance depends on making ourselves acceptable we will be more interested in doing what is acceptable than what is truly helpful. In some societies the giving of alms to beggars has two important functions in making people acceptable. The beggar makes himself acceptable by showing his humility in begging. The person who bestows gifts upon him makes himself acceptable by demonstrating his generosity. Begging allows both the beggar and the almsgiver to please God. Thus the humiliating and embarrassing practice of begging is perpetuated. If you know that you are accepted, you can ask what course of action would be most helpful in avoiding the need to beg, and actually help people who may be handicapped live decent lives without the need for constant humiliation.

When you have accepted your acceptance you are free to serve God in the neighbor without trying to establish a case for your charity in the sight of God. In accepting God's acceptance you are freed from self-concern and can thank God without embarrassment for all the gifts he has so graciously bestowed upon you. "In Christ Jesus, then, I have reason to be proud of my work for God. For I will not venture to speak of anything except what Christ has wrought through me." This is the relaxed attitude of the Christian lifestyle, not clutching for appreciation and gratitude, but thanking God that he has used us to serve him.

22

The Christian Lifestyle

Who is a Christian? How would you answer this question after reading Paul's letter to the Romans and these chapters based on Paul's letter? How would Paul have answered this question? What does the question mean? If you turn to *Webster's New International Dictionary* you receive a number of clues. The first meaning given says: "One who believes or professes or is assumed to believe, in Jesus Christ, and the truth as taught by Him; an adherent of Christianity. Esp., one who has definitely accepted the Christian religious and moral principles of life; one who has faith in and has pledged allegiance to God, thought of as revealed in Christ; one whose life is conformed to the doctrine of Christ." The emphasis in this definition is clearly on the acceptance of principles and life in conformity with doctrines. Here a Christian is a person who sees things a certain way. Christianity seems to be a point of view, a perspective on life.

But the dictionary gives us many definitions. We can ignore the second meaning, where Christian is "a masculine proper name." But the third meaning is again of real interest: "3a, *Now chiefly dial.*, a human being as distinguished from one of the lower animals." Even if "chiefly dialect," it tells us that for some people at least the term "Christian" is synonymous with "human." Even if Paul never used the word in this sense, and most of us would find such use both pretentious and misleading, it hints at some of the implications of what Paul has been trying to tell us. Potentially everybody is a Christian; no human being is excluded from this community by God, who wants all people to be saved. Some theologians may have seen this differently (e.g., Calvin), but we would have to admit that nothing we read in Romans 12-15 would lead us to believe that there is any human being who is not potentially a Christian.

This amazing inclusiveness of the Christian movement as described by Paul has repeatedly been brought to our attention. But meaning 3 has a subheading *b*: "*Colloq.*, A decent civilized, respectable, or presentable person." There is no doubt that "colloquially" Christian means for many people precisely what the dictionary says here, and this is a serious problem for all Christians. It is this definition which makes the church the stodgy, even exclusive, middle-class institution which you can't enter unless you think of yourself in the terms of this definition, which means at least that you wear decent clothes and are not obviously in trouble. This definition may have no theological significance at all, but for the view of the Christian lifestyle of most people it is this description which has been decisive. It is the view of the church which has kept many people out and which explains why, according to every statistical survey, membership in the church is highly correlated to income. The poorer you are, the less likely it is that you will find yourself a "Christian" in this perverse sense of the word. What would Paul have said about this definition?

But there is still another definition: "4. One born in a Christian country or of Christian parents who has not definitely adhered to an opposing system." This definition is almost identical with the definition of a "Jew" given by a ruling of the Supreme Court of the state of Israel. The court held that a Jew is a person born of a Jewish mother who has not accepted another religion. By this definition an atheist could be a Jew, but a person who obeyed the Jewish law to the letter, but believed that Jesus is the Messiah, would not be a Jew. It is a strangely negative definition, but in many parts of the world, particularly in many countries in Europe, it is in common usage: You are a Christian unless you are something else. In countries like the United States the term "Protestant" tends to be used in this way: If you aren't a Roman Catholic or a Jew, you are Protestant, whether you like it or not. Such a definition makes no demands at all. For a man like Paul it would be incomprehensible.

The dictionary has still other definitions, including one referring to the members of a particular denomination which by means of adopting the name "Christian" for their denomination wanted to unite all followers of Christ into one church and abolish denominationalism. Predictably, the result was one more denomination. Other definitions which apply to other cultures are not even mentioned in the dictionary. In some countries, to say, "I am a Christian," may mean that you want to indicate that you are an educated person, since Christianity is identified with the most highly developed educational system in these countries.

None of these definitions do justice to Paul's description of the Christian lifestyle in Romans 12-15. For him it is not the mere acceptance of certain doctrines or life in conformity with such doctrines. It is certainly not respectability in opinion or dress. Nor is it the same as citizenship in some earthly kingdom or republic. For Paul the Christian lifestyle means something that has been given to the Christian by God and which he may accept, even if he considers himself unworthy of the gift. But the gift God gives to each person is tailored to the needs of that man, woman, or child, and thus a little different and special for each individual. Christians are not mass-produced; they are Spirit-crafted, and the differences are seen as an advantage.

The resulting lifestyle is based on faith, hope, and love, and all three gifts of the Spirit must be put to work in the world. The perspective for this work is that "he who loves his neighbor has fulfilled the law" (Rom. 13:8). "The night is far gone, the day is at hand. Let us then cast off the works of darkness and put on the armor of light" (Rom. 13:12-13).

Notes

Page

21 BENEDICT: Ruth Benedict in her *Patterns of Culture* (New York: New American Library, 1946) analyzes the culture of the Zunis, Pueblo Indians in New Mexico; Dobuans, living on an island off the southern shore of eastern New Guinea; and Kwakiutls, who lived on Vancouver Island on the narrow strip of Pacific seacoast from Alaska to Puget Sound.

21 SOLZHENITSYN: In *The Gulag Archipelago, 1918-1956* (New York: Harper & Row, 1973) Aleksandr I. Solzhenitsyn describes this system of police terror in the U.S.S.R. which reached its peak under Stalin.

29 MILGRAM: The experiment here related was reported by Stanley Milgram in *Obedience to Authority: An Experimental View* (New York: Harper & Row, 1974).

33 KANT: Immanuel Kant, as quoted in *The Philosophy of Kant: Immanuel Kant's Moral and Political Writings,* ed. Carl J. Friedrich (New York: The Modern Library, 1949), p. 222.

34 PHILO: Philo Judaeus (ca. 25 B.C. to 45 A.D.) was the Jewish philosopher who combined the Old Testament tradition with the ideas of the Hellenistic world. The quotation is from his book *The Decalogue,* par. 87, in *Philo,* with an English translation by I. H. Cason, 9 vols. (Cambridge: Harvard University Press, 1937), 7:51.

41 A PHYSCHIATRIST . . . REPORTED: See Victor E. Frankl, *Man's Search for Meaning* (New York: Washington Square Press, 1963).

41 BLOCH: In his book *Das Prinzip Hoffnung* (Frankfurt: Suhrkamp, 1959) Ernst Bloch distinguishes between daydreams and night dreams; note esp. pp. 85-101.

65 OPPENHEIMER: The distinguished physicist J. Robert Oppenheimer in a lecture entitled "Physics in the Contemporary World" delivered at the Massachusetts Institute of Technology on November 25, 1947.

70 DE UNAMUNO: Miguel de Unamuno, *The Agony of Christianity,* trans. Kurt F. Reinhardt (New York: Frederick Ungar, 1960), p. 19.

74   BUTTERFIELD: Herbert Butterfield, Professor of Modern History at the University of Cambridge, in his *Christianity and History* (London: Fontana Books, 1957), p. 189.

74   LUTHER: See the American Edition of *Luther's Works* (Philadelphia and St. Louis, 1955—   ), 35:396.

78   CELSUS: As quoted by Origen in *Origen Against Celsus, Ante-Nicene Fathers* (New York: Scribner's, 1926), 7:481.

82   SANDBURG: Carl Sandburg in the poem "Prairie" in *Cornhuskers* (New York: Henry Holt, 1918), p. 11.

84   WEBSTER'S . . . DICTIONARY: *Webster's New International Dictionary of the English Language*, 2d ed., unabridged (Springfield, Mass.: G. & C. Merriam Co., 1961).